Helping
CHILDREN
of
DIVORCE

Judson J. Swihart
& Steven L. Brigham

InterVarsity Press
Downers Grove
Illinois 60515

© 1982 by Inter-Varsity Christian Fellowship of the United States of America

InterVarsity Press is the book-publishing division of Inter-Varsity Christian
Fellowship, a student movement active on campus at hundreds of universities,
colleges and schools of nursing. For information about local and regional
activities, write IVCF, 233 Langdon St., Madison, WI 53703.

Distributed in Canada through InterVarsity Press, 1875 Leslie St., Unit 10,
Don Mills, Ontario M3B 2M5, Canada.

ISBN 0-87784-373-2

Printed in the United States of America

Library of Congress Cataloging in Publication Data

Swihart, Judson J.
    Helping children of divorce.

    Bibliography: p.

    1. Children of divorced parents—Psychology.
2. Parent and child.   I. Brigham, Steven L.
II. Title.

| HQ777.5.S96 | 1982 | 306.8'74 | 82-8945 |
| ISBN 0-87784-373-2 | | | AACR2 |

| 14 | 13 | 12 | 11 | 10 | 9 | 8 | 7 | 6 | 5 | 4 | 3 | 2 | 1 |
| 93 | 92 | 91 | 90 | 89 | 88 | 87 | 86 | 85 | 84 | 83 | 82 |

*We dedicate this book to Mandy Brigham
and Nancy Swihart along with Derrick,
Dan and Sara Swihart for providing us with
experiences that have helped us to
understand human relationships better.*

*We also thank Pat Hayes and Fran Watkins
for typing assistance, Mitchell Thomas
for editorial comments, and all three for helpful
suggestions throughout the manuscript.
We would like to thank Lauren Glen Dunlap
who contributed greatly to our story
"Something to Cry About."*

Surviving Divorce

*If there is anything that we wish
to change in the child, we should first
examine it and see whether it is
not something that could better be
changed in ourselves.*
—Carl Gustav Jung

1

"Divorce is one of the most serious and complex mental health crises facing children in the 1980's."[1] Those words of Albert Solnit, director of the Yale Child Study Center, reflect the increasingly significant impact that divorce is having on American family life.

From 1950 to 1980 the divorce rate in the United States more than doubled.[2] Since 1972 an additional one million children each year have been affected by their parents' divorce. Approximately forty-five per cent of the children currently growing up in the United States will see the separation or divorce of their parents.[3] In a group of new-born infants at any local hospital one could reasonably expect that half of them will be raised by a single parent.

In a divorce, children may not only lose a parent; they may also as a result of relocation lose their home, school and friends. Because the parent they live with often works outside the home, they experience more time alone and more time with other caretakers. For many children divorce means economic hardship. If the remaining parent begins to date, children can be thrown into further confusion and turmoil. Although they react in different ways, many experience feelings of insecurity, guilt, anger and depression. Some will doubt the remaining parent's love for them. Nearly all cling to a futile hope of reuniting their family, though this is likely to never occur.

Yet children survive the divorce and life continues. For some it is more difficult than for others. Major elements of adjustment include parental reactions, children's perceptions of the divorce and the support they get from others. The purpose of this book is to help parents, relatives, friends and teachers assist children in the difficult adjustments to divorce.

Working through Divorce

A recent study surveying a number of children several years after their family's divorce found that they had one of three experiences. One-third of the children interviewed came through the divorce successfully; they ended up with positive self-images and had good outlooks on life. Another third muddled through, experiencing many difficulties and some successes. The last third never recovered from the trauma and hence continued hurt and injured, always hoping and wishing that things could go back as they were.[4] It is our hope that these chapters will enable parents, grandparents, relatives, friends, schoolteachers and others to help children improve their chances of joining the ranks of those who come through divorce successfully adjusted.

The issue of divorce is controversial among Christians. Some believe that divorce is not proper under any circumstances. Others believe that divorce is acceptable only when adultery has occurred. Still others accept divorce if one spouse has inflicted acute physical or psychological harm on the other. A minority think that divorce should be an option for anyone who is not currently content and satisfied in his or her marriage. Regardless of one's position on that issue, we cannot disregard the reality that divorces are occurring and, given human nature, will most likely continue to occur.

Children in the church often experience a subtle condemnation from church members if their parents are divorced. Even if a church member believes that a child's parents' divorce is not biblically warranted, one must remember that divorce was not the choice of the child.

We are concerned that some might misinterpret this book as an encouragement of divorce. That is not correct. We have spent many years in professional training, research and professional counseling, helping families to adjust, cope and grow strong in the flow of everyday life. We desire to see families flourish as a building block of our society, yet reality tells us that this does not always occur. This book is written out of the reality of our counseling. We see a need to help children who did not choose divorce, but who are part of a system that dictates this change in their life. Thus, we emphasize, this book does not intend to sanction divorce, but instead tries to offer healing solutions to children affected by divorce.

While adjustment to divorce is considered from a biblical perspective, we could not find biblical models to follow when it comes to discussing such adjustment. Divorce occurred in both Old and New Testament days, yet the problem of the children involved is not specifically addressed. Hosea, for example, went through a time of separation, but we do not know the reaction of his children. There are, however, biblical models of children raised apart from their families: Moses and Samuel. God honored both; certainly it did not mean the end of God's favor for them.

Growth through Pain

One theme of this book is that growth can come through painful situations. Although spiritual growth does not always come through pain, we believe that every painful situation has potential for spiritual growth. People are most likely to turn to God when confronted with situations they cannot easily handle on their own. If one does turn to God, this painful experience can also be a time to know his comfort and his help. Thus faith can be strengthened.

A close friend went through a trying divorce a number

of years ago. At first many people had told Maria she had to accept the reality of what was happening. But at that point, the pain was too great. She couldn't accept what was happening to her. As she grew in her trust in God, however, and saw his daily provision, he brought that acceptance. At the time Maria didn't realize the healing that was taking place in her life; only in retrospect can she look back and see what happened. Those who know her can sense the growth that came through that harsh situation. Her life is a model for others who face similar situations. The key was that instead of becoming bitter Maria sought and found closeness with God.

Some of the situations we describe in these chapters will not be relevant to every family. At the same time, so many combinations of factors are involved in divorce that it is impossible to address them all. In some divorces both husband and wife want the divorce. In others one doesn't want it, yet it is forced on him or her. Sometimes children from a previous marriage are in the picture. Other times there are no children. In some situations one spouse is a Christian and the other is not. Other times neither or both are Christians. In addition, some parents faithfully visit the children and others never see them again, with all other variations in between. Add to this the distinct personalities of the people involved, and you begin to get a picture of the complexity of divorce. In our illustrations, we have tried not to be overly idealistic, yet not to assume the worst either. We hope our readers will adapt the principles to the circumstances they know.

Telling Children

*Making terms with reality,
with things as they are, is a
full-time business for the child.*
—*Milton R. Sapirstein*

2

When people decide to separate, one big question always arises. What should they tell their children? Although every situation is different, certain guidelines should be considered.

Divorce is a decision that first affects two people. Both mother and father should plan when, where and how to discuss their decision with the children. What will be said by whom, or at least some format of procedures should be agreed on beforehand. A prepared speech is not necessary; rather, a direction should be established with which both husband and wife can feel comfortable.

Some parents prefer to tell each child separately, so

they can adapt the details of the explanation to different age levels. On the other hand, it may be best to tell all the children at the same time since that allows them to give support to each other. This also avoids their coming in one at a time and then leaving, feeling they are alone in knowing a terrible secret. By talking to all of them together, the children know exactly what has been said and can clarify misconceptions with each other as they discuss it later among themselves. Parents sometimes avoid this because it is painful; they fear that they themselves may break into tears. Yet being able to see the parents' tears, in fact, may be a useful model for the children in dealing with their own grief.

Toddlers are unable to form verbal questions and cannot ask the reason for one parent's absence. Nor can they understand a description of why their father or mother does not come home on a regular basis. Children who can verbalize reasonably well should be told about the separation and be given opportunities to discuss it in detail. The discussion needs to be general as well as sensitive to the developmental level of the child. Even toddlers realize that their parent is not there and should be told that he is living in another place where he sleeps and eats.

What Do You Say?

The best approach in telling children about a divorce is straightforward honesty.[1] A great deal of confusion is created when children are first told something like, "Your father is away on a business trip and won't be home for a while." It is much better to present the decision directly.

While some parents think this will be a shock to their children, it often is not a surprise at all. The decision to divorce is usually the culmination of a long process of conflict. Invariably the children have sensed the tension even when it is not open and direct. Before one couple's decision to seek a divorce was announced, their five-year-old told the grandmother, "I don't think Daddy and Mommy love each other anymore." Such awareness is not at all unusual.

A small child of three or four cannot understand long explanations about their mother and father separating or words like "irreconcilable differences." Older children, however, can understand a more detailed explanation. For example: "Your dad and I have had a difficult time in our marriage. We both have had needs that the other has not been able to meet. Our relationship has never grown over the years, and now I am almost totally uninvolved with your father. If you ask him, I think he'll tell you that he sees our marriage the same way." The major point, then, is to tell all children in the family, even toddlers, about the impending action but to base your discussion on their level of understanding.

Many children are not told enough. A study conducted in California found that eighty per cent of preschoolers whose parents were separating had received no explanation.[2] That is a very significant statistic when viewed from the perspective of the child's self-understanding; one of the two most important people in his or her life is no longer

17

going to be living with the family. The concept that "they are too young to know" does not seem consistent with what we know about early childhood development. Children can begin to understand and process simple information at an early age.

The explanation should also make the point that although the parents are choosing to live separately, it does not mean they will stop loving the children. In fact, parents should assure their children that they were wanted at birth, are still wanted and will have a continuing relationship with each parent—assuming that all those factors are true and are not just platitudes to alleviate the pain. Common questions like "Will Dad stop loving me since he's stopped loving Mom?" and "Will Mom stop loving me since she's stopped loving Dad?" indicate that children struggle with issues about love and security within relationships. Often it is useful to spend time talking with the children about the similarities and dissimilarities of love between adults and parent-child love.

Don't involve the children in a power struggle.[3] They should not be asked to take sides or agree with one parent or the other. Attempts to fix blame have adverse consequences on children. Put in the middle, children are in a no-win position.

Sometimes parents differ on the issue of lifestyle or values. A father, for example, may leave his home, denounce his previous Christian values, and assume a promiscuous lifestyle which the children are fully aware of. In such a situation a mother may choose to teach her children about a God who loves us in spite of our behavior. She can also choose to discuss with the children the vast differences in values without causing the children to have to choose sides between parents.

When is the best time to tell children so as to minimize the trauma associated with such a disclosure? Unless there are special circumstances, it is usually better to tell them a few days to a week before parents actually separate. Telling them, of course, assumes a final decision to separate has been made and confirmed. If there is indecision, wait until a final decision is made. A few days' to a week's notice will give children sufficient time to prepare themselves emotionally for the separation, yet not a long time for them to dwell on it. It is much better for them to have time to adjust to the divorce or separation rather than to come home from school and find that their father is no longer living there. The latter creates anxiety about future losses that might also catch them unaware.

Parents' Anger

The divorces discussed so far may seem somewhat amiable; that, for the most part, is more a hope than a reality. Whenever parents divorce, the situation is generally charged with anger. The more the children can be protected from this, the better it is for everyone. Although parents need to be able to experience their feelings, there needs to be some containment of anger when the children are present.

It is important not to berate the spouse in front of the

children. Even if not verbalized, children perceive the anger. The idea is to protect them from being flooded by it. For several reasons children should be left out of as much of the parents' anger as possible. First, seeing two people you love so distraught with each other intensifies their emotion and magnifies their insecurity. They may feel they need to choose sides, which creates further conflicts in them. Some children transfer to themselves the putdowns of their parents and in so doing reduce their own self-esteem.

Likewise, the spouse should not be overpraised to protect the children. If, as part of the description of the reasons for separation, one parent excessively praises the other, that may create questions for the children like, "If the other person is so wonderful, why are you getting a divorce?" It also gives them concern for themselves and their acceptance by that parent, even when that person reassures them. Describe the causes, making it very clear to the children that they are not the cause of the divorce.

Dealing with Insecurity

Children may wonder what happens to the spouse who is leaving. Where does Mom or Dad go? If they are preschool children, they may even envision that the spouse is disappearing. So it is useful for the children to accompany their father to his new room, apartment or wherever he is staying. (This assumes he will be living in the area and keeping in contact with the children.) By doing this, they actually see where their parent lives, the kind of furniture he or she has and what the rooms look like. Such a visit will decrease some of the children's anxiety about the separation.

Sometimes, however, such a visit may prove embarrassing—at least to the other parent. For example, in one family, the father had a two-bedroom apartment, with one room rented out to a female companion. When the children visited, this raised questions rather than decreasing anxiety.

Ready accessibility of the departed spouse can lessen the trauma. By telephoning or writing the children, visiting them often or having them over, the parent maintains important continuity. It is helpful to give the children his or her phone number on a paper or card that they can carry with them or keep in a convenient place. That way they know how to reach their parent (assuming he or she is available by phone) and feel a sense of access to that parent.

Children's Initial Reactions

Initial reaction to being told of the separation is not always what might be expected. Sometimes it is quiet; other times there is an emotional outburst. The usual first response may not demonstrate emotion because denial of such an event is strong. When children's reaction to the announcement that their father or mother won't be living there anymore is one of calm, the parents may wonder if they really care very much. In reality, their inner reaction may be disbelief. "This can't really be happening." Or, "They won't go through with this."[4] Denial can last a long time. Depending on the age of the children, they sometimes fantasize that their father is just at work. Or, if between the ages of two and four, children may fantasize that their mother is still there watching her favorite television program with them. Parents should understand the effects of such a denial and not measure children's relationship to the departing parent by the emotion they initially demonstrate.

Sarah, age six, whose father had died one year previously, said that her daddy was away at work and had just not come home yet. Intellectually she knew he would not return, but emotionally she was still denying it to ward off her painful feelings. The child of divorce needs reassurance that although Dad has moved out, he or others will continue to provide the love the child needs. If that reassurance is true, such consolation should be offered. But if not, if the departing parent leaves permanently, false reassurance should not be given.

No Role Shifting

When talking to children about the divorce, it is better not to allow them to shift roles or to increase your expectations of them. They should be allowed to remain children in the relationship. To say to the oldest boy in the house, "Now that Daddy has left us, you are going to be the man of the house," creates considerable pressure for the boy at a time when he is trying to adjust to the loss of his father.

It also creates emotional difficulties for him to deal with in "replacing the father," particularly if there was any previous rivalry for the mother's attention in the family. Ecclesiastes 3 indicates a natural time or season for all things. It shows the creation and design in the universe. When things are moved out of their "season," problems result.

A teen-ager, Nancy, had been placed in the role of surrogate parent because her mother was gone much of the time. The younger children began taking out their frustrations toward both parents on her. She soon began developing physical symptoms, including stomach and neck aches, because of the stress. Childhood, including adolescence, is a season that should be left in its natural state. While it is good for the remaining parent to share his or her feelings with the children, divorce is not a time to unload burdens on them or place them in positions of responsibility too great for them.

Should the Teacher and Physician Be Told?

Because children are likely to react to the divorce in the school environment, their teachers should be told about the home situation, especially for preadolescent children. That allows the teachers to be alert to changes in the child and to help as needed. Older children may rely more on peers for support, whereas for younger children the teacher is often the most significant other person in their life. If the child is in need of medical care, the physician should be told. Some physical symptoms could be related to the feelings the child is dealing with at that time.

Is There a Good Time to Divorce?

Parents often wonder about staying together for the children's sake or possibly postponing divorce until the children are older. If they have really decided to separate, when should they do so? This question assumes that the children's needs are of prime consideration and that the suffering the parents are experiencing is of secondary importance.

Unless the parents wait until all the children are grown, there usually is no really good time for separation. Usually there are children at various developmental stages in the family. When, for example, there is a girl three to five years old, some professionals argue that the loss of her father deprives her of a male figure at a point in her life when she is forming concepts that will affect the way she relates to men.[5] For a little boy, they argue that he may feel guilt over his father's leaving because this is an age when he is particularly attached to his mother. Others advise not to separate at a time when children are starting school because that means two separations at once. Some theorists believe that parents' separating during early adolescence could mean that the boy will not have a father with whom to identify and the daughter will not develop relational skills with the opposite sex.[6] There does not seem to be any ideal time, although many professionals believe that the earlier the trauma in the child's life, the greater the distress.

These are problems parents face and wonder about in the process of divorce. They are difficult issues that do not have easy or pleasant answers. When possible, however, they need to be dealt with in a way that minimizes the trauma for the children.

Crisis through the Eyes of Children

Children are remarkable for their intelligence and ardor, for their curiosity, their intolerance of slams, the clarity and ruthlessness of their vision.
—Aldous Huxley

3

When a divorce or separation is taking place, it is important to understand how that phenomenon appears in the child's eyes. "When I was a child, I understood as a child." As parents, it is useful to be able to walk a mile in your children's shoes.

Once children have realized that their parents are separating or divorcing, they enter a state of crisis. The usual coping mechanisms no longer are able to provide a sense of well-being. Children often feel that things are out of control. They cannot by their behavior pull together their crumbling world. That feeling of helplessness tends to increase the sense of crisis.

Parents often think there will not be a crisis since the home was previously loaded with tension. They believe that through a divorce the children will gain a sense of relief from the anxiety in the home. But a recent study has shown that less than ten per cent of the children experienced relief at the time of separation even though thirty per cent had witnessed scenes of physical violence between their parents. Five years after the divorce, over fifty per cent of the children did not consider their family life improved over what it had been prior to the divorce. Although their parents had been unhappy, the children were fairly happy and did not believe they were any worse off than other families. The parents felt relief from the divorce, but the children's psychological health did not markedly improve.[1]

We all initially deny a crisis. Children persist in their idea that their parents will get back together simply because the idea of their parents' separating or divorcing is too painful for them to accept. One study found that initially nearly all children have fantasies about their parents' reuniting or that everything will be fine again.[2] That may be true in some cases, but in many cases it is not. If the children are clinging to that type of hope when, in fact, there is no hope, it may be better for the parent to remind them gently that the separation or divorce is, in fact, going to take place.

When you talk with the children about the crisis, the most useful format is to keep focused on the here and now rather than spending a lot of time going on and on about what has happened in the past. It is useful to convey to them the expectation that although the marriage relationship has ended, there will be many happy times in the future. You can specifically describe the kinds of things they should be able to do with each parent.

Realizing the facts of the situation is necessary before children can complete their adjustment. As long as they are holding out hope of reconciliation, it is difficult, if not impossible, for them to adjust to the loss of their intact family. For some children, however, that loss may be too much to accept. The confirmation that their parents will never live together again is devastating to them. These children need time before they can adjust to the new realities that confront them, so the issue should not be forced on them.

Listening is important. Parents need to understand what ideas and concepts the children may have about the future. For example, a boy may be telling himself that he will never see his father again or will never be happy again. He may be thinking he will never have any more good times with his father, when in fact the father may intend to see him several times a week and consistently have good input into his life.

Parents need to keep several background factors in mind in minimizing the crisis. First, one must consider the amount of change a child faces in adjusting to a divorce. Although part of the experience is the loss of one parent at home, it also may mean that the family has a sense of isolation. Old friends may avoid social contact, fearing to be caught in the middle. Maybe the divorcing parents are less comfortable around married friends and find it painful going to social events with friends who are couples. The children therefore have less exposure to family friends whom they also enjoyed and from whom they gained support.

Sometimes the divorce may mean a change of neighborhood. That may mean the loss of families, surroundings and playmates for the child. Sometimes there are several children and the children are shuffled back and forth. Sometimes the family sells the home to divide community property. Or a child may go to live with the father in a new area. Such changes may result in a new school. Many times the separation means a change in child-care arrangements. Perhaps Mom now needs to work outside the home, or maybe work schedules are changed so new arrangements are made. The child now adjusts to being alone more or having a new baby sitter.

Another part of the change is that often less money will be available. The family now has the expense of two households. Many times fathers do not or are not able to contribute to the former level of support. One study determined that the average support for children of divorced parents was less than half the usual cost considered generally necessary for raising children.[3] The child now has fewer new clothes, new toys and opportunities for piano, gymnastics or art lessons.

With all those changes occurring, a useful plan is for parents to stabilize as much of the environment as possible. Try to leave the children in the same school and make an effort to continue family routines to give a sense of stability.

Another important factor is giving children ready access to yourself as a parent and to other adults who are significant in their lives. Significant people include grandparents, friends, relatives and neighbors to whom they can talk and from whom they can receive support.

Children experience several fairly common reactions in dealing with the process of separation and divorce. Here we will discuss some of those responses in a general way. More specific reactions and their dynamics will be considered in chapters four and five.

Was I Bad?

The first major reaction is that children wonder why this important person in their life is leaving. Usually behind that question is their concern over what part they played in this. "What did I do to cause Dad to leave?" (Here we refer to the father since usually he is the one who moves out, and the children stay with the mother. But the frequency rate is changing.) Children tend to blame themselves for their parents' relationship coming apart. That may not make much sense on a rational level to the parents; the child, however, may feel very much at fault. And doesn't it make sense that if you caused the divorce, it was because you were bad? Younger children particularly feel this way because they look at events in terms of good and bad.

One family had a seven-year-old girl who had run away from home several times. The last time Monica ran away from home she complicated things by taking her four-year-old brother with her. The family was trying to understand why the little girl was doing this. It was the mother's second marriage, and the children were hers from her previous marriage.

As counseling progressed, it was discovered that the mother and stepfather were having some fairly severe arguments. They reported, however, that the children did not know about the arguments because they never argued in front of them. Upon further exploration, it was found that Monica had overheard, had felt that she was the one causing the marital problems, and had concluded that it was better for her to leave the family rather than be responsible for her parents' splitting up. She still had some self-blame for her mother's first divorce. With the parents' participation in marriage counseling, along with Monica's own realization that she was not the cause of the parents' problems, the symptom of running away soon terminated.

Children often make the assumption that they have somehow been bad although they are not exactly sure how. Self-blame may manifest itself in a direct statement, such as, "I wish I were a better kid so that Dad wouldn't have left." Reprimands for misbehavior during this time tend to confirm them in that line of thought.

Other signs of self-condemnation may indicate that the child feels guilty for what happened in the marriage. Sometimes it results in a depressive response. The child mopes a lot and doesn't seem to enjoy play.

Sometimes the outward expression of "I'm bad" goes in the opposite direction, which takes even more sensitivity to deal with. Children may think, "Since my being bad created problems, what can I do to try to hold this family together?" The children may become super-good. They will be very cooperative. At times they will beg mother and father not to go through with the divorce but to come back together. If being bad pulled the marriage apart, then being super-good should put it together again.

Children may also fear that if they are bad, they will be left. This is more likely to happen if the parent who has left had exhibited behaviors like excessive drinking, infidelity or irresponsibility.

Letting go of guilt can be complicated for children whose parents have always seemed right and perfect. When parents project that image to their children, children are likely to judge that they themselves must be the ones at fault. Since the parents are perfect, they obviously can't be blamed.

Embarrassment

A second feeling that is often present for those who live in a very pro-family setting is embarrassment about divorce. Because divorce goes against everything that these people stand for, the children feel they won't be accepted. That is especially the case when one of the parents has been involved in a scandal. Suppose it is widely known that the wife has been routinely having affairs or that the husband's gambling has caused the family to lose their home or that she was involved in a major company fraud. The child is certainly going to be vulnerable to a sense of embarrassment from those circumstances. If the parents are active in the church or have held strong beliefs, the parents may feel embarrassed about the divorce. Children often experience their parents' feelings.

Sometimes a judgment and condemnation process actually takes place with some Christians or some churches. (Other times the judgments may be more in the perception of the divorced person than in reality.) Christ asks us not to judge or condemn others. He did not condemn the woman about to be stoned for adultery when her accusers had left. The church community needs to offer forgiveness, be supportive and bring healing. Yet often it is the last place Christians turn for support when they are divorcing or separating. We need to explore ways in which churches can eliminate the embarrassment for both parents and children who feel as though they have failed yet need encouragement more than ever.

One youth pastor's wife left him just prior to a major church function. As part of the pastoral staff he felt compelled to give other reasons for his wife's absence. If there was ever a time when he needed the ministry of others it was then, yet the need to live up to expectations was so great for him that he covered things as long as he could. If being restrained by great feelings of embarrassment occurs with adults, it seems even more tragic in the lives of children.

34

Insecurity and Dependence

Third, to some extent nearly all children of divorce are insecure. Because they now live with one parent, they fear what would happen to them if abandoned by that parent. Fear of being alone in the world is at the core of the perceived danger.

Many people deal with this same issue all their lives. They reveal their fear by their unwillingness to fight, trying hard to please others who could potentially reject them. They feel unable to confront others. With that awareness about adults, you can begin to sense the measure of fear in a young child who has just lost one parent. Therefore, at the time of separation or divorce, it is good to talk to the children about who exactly would take care of them. Reassurance and a well-reasoned plan should exist, such as, "If I become sick and can't take care of you, then Grandmother and Grandfather would take care of you, or Uncle Mike and Aunt Susie," and so on.

Children also need to be dependent although they sometimes protest loudly that they don't. Given the insecurity of their world, the need for dependence often becomes obvious, especially in younger children. Clinging, always wanting to be in the same room, not going to visit friends, or not even wanting to go to school for fear Mom or Dad won't be there when the child gets back— all are signs of extreme dependence. Sometimes, however, these needs are blurred by other factors, such as parents seeking to fulfill their own dependency needs.

Divorce or separation is a time of life when children

learn they can control some things and not others. To learn that is difficult, but such a time can also provide opportunity to learn that things get worked out even when they are not in control. With older children a parent might discuss the story of Joseph and how he was sold into slavery. God had a special plan for Joseph's life and was still in control even though it might not have looked that way to him at the time.

A couple was separated and filing for divorce. Ginny reported that her daughter, Ellen, was afraid to be alone at night. Being a concerned mother, Ginny arranged for a night light to be left on so the child could see where she was, should she awaken in fear. Although the light helped, it wasn't until Ellen's father spent more time with her that her fear subsided.

Fear of abandonment does not always show up early in the separation. One study showed that during the first two months of separation fathers were as involved with their children as much as ever and in some cases were spending more time with them than prior to the divorce. After that, however, there was a steady decline in attention to the children, and for many fathers, after two years, there was a significant decrease in the amount of time spent as well as in the quality of the relationship.[4] For those children, therefore, fear of abandonment may not show up until later.

Children feel a sense of loss of the family structure that served as a protection against the world. That is particularly the case with a child who felt very secure with a father who is now absent. Children also worry about the distress which they sense their parents are going through. Such worry, of course, varies with the amount of distress and how much of it is presented to the child.

Anger and Depression

Mixed with fear is often an anger which children feel they cannot express. They may be very angry at their parent for leaving the family, but are unable to communicate the anger because of fear of driving him or her further away and losing even more security. Children then may become depressed. One study by McDermott showed that about one-third of the children of separated parents were depressed, showing little spontaneity or exuberance. They seemed serious and devoid of happiness and joy. Some had those obvious symptoms of depression. Others had self-destructive fantasies or became accident-prone.[5]

Grief and Mourning

Another problem is children's sense of loss and resulting grief. Experts differ over whether or not young children mourn in the sense of confronting their pain. Some believe fairly young children do mourn; others think actual mourning does not take place until sometime around adolescence.[6] Before adolescence these experts perceive crying as an attempt to retrieve the missing parent, not as a result of letting go or dealing with their loss.

We believe, however, that all children experience some sense of pain, regardless of what developmental stage

37

they are in and will express that pain in some form of grief. The biggest factor may well be the support of significant people in allowing children to grieve. The grief process needs careful attention and support from others because children who are not allowed to deal with their pain may well carry it into adulthood where it has potential for being disruptive.

Age Differences

Age is also an important factor in the way different reactions and emotions are expressed. A five-year California study of children from divorced families found that within particular age groups children had fairly predictable responses. Among younger children, preschoolers and kindergarteners, regression was a common way of handling feelings concerning their parents' separation. Children would move back to an earlier level of functioning where things were more comfortable. Also common in that age group were certain symptoms of depression: children were often irritable, whining, crying and fearful. For some children there were sleep problems, aggressive behavior and tantrums.[7]

The same study found that six-to-ten-year-olds often exhibited a rather intense sadness. This arose from loyalty and longing for the absent parent, even when the relationship was not particularly close.

Although grief is still there, it may not be so strong a reaction in children under twelve because of their inability to understand the amount of loss. Grief can also be

Figure 1
Divorce Adjustment Factors

Lessens Impact of Divorce	Increases Impact of Divorce
1. Parents do not put children in the middle.	1. Children are asked to choose between parents.
2. Children are told about the separation.	2. Children are not told about separation or are given little information.
3. Children are aware of the conflict between parents.	3. Parents hide conflict and angry feelings.
4. Children are not held responsible for the divorce.	4. Children are made to feel that divorce is their fault.
5. Children are not used for parental support.	5. Parent relies on child for personal support.
6. Children receive support from significant people.	6. Children are isolated from family friends.
7. Parents resolve personal anger.	7. Parents are unable to resolve anger.
8. The absent parent stays in contact with the child.	8. The absent parent has little contact with child.
9. Siblings.	9. Only child.
10. Family moves into new schedule fairly quickly.	10. Family remains disorganized long after separation.
11. Other environmental factors remain stable.	11. Life is greatly changed: school, neighborhood, parent's work hours and so on.
12. Each parent frequently spends individual time with each child.	12. Little individual attention is given to children.
13. Parents assist each child with individual adjustment reaction.	13. Parents are not aware of individual adjustment reactions.
14. Children are allowed to grieve.	14. Loss is denied—no grieving is allowed.
15. Family focuses on the positive and the future.	15. Family focuses on present calamity.
16. Parents had previous good relationship with child.	16. Child had not previously felt loved or valued by parents.

cloaked by denial. "Now that Dad has left, things will be a lot better around here; now I can watch any TV show I want and not have to sit through his ball games." This age group, however, has many fears of being abandoned or forgotten by the parent who has left.

The study showed that nine- to twelve-year-olds worried about the same things as younger children. But in this group the feelings were less intense since older children are often more openly angry at the parents. Younger children evidently tend more frequently to blame themselves for the parents' separating or divorcing than older children.

Adolescents are old enough to sort through the reasons for the divorce and have less tendency to blame themselves. They are able to leave home to spend more time with their friends and thus have more social support and contacts. Their mobility enables them to cope better with the distress they feel. Children of this age are also more observant and consequently are concerned about their parents' adjustment to the divorce.

Various factors can have a marked effect on children's adjustment to divorce. Figure 1 summarizes some factors that can lessen or increase the impact of divorce on children.

Common Reactions in Children

To every action there is always opposed an equal reaction.
—Sir Isaac Newton

4

Nobody fits exactly into rigid categories or pigeonholes. We are not merely "types." God has made each of us unique, and in life we tend to develop that uniqueness. In studying human nature, however, psychologists and other researchers and theorists have described a number of patterns of human behavior. All individuals reflect characteristics of several or all of these categories. Some patterns are apt to crop up and become more visible for a while when children (or adults) are under stress. Here we will itemize particular ways that children may respond to divorce. Our intent is not to make divorced parents feel forever guilty about the way their children turn out. Neither the divorce nor the parents themselves are the cause of every subsequent behavioral problem in their children's lives.

Showoffs

"Little showoffs" are children who deal with the stress of divorce by becoming boastful, boisterous and rambunctious. They perform tricks. They want you to watch them. Depending on age level, this may be anything from turning somersaults to riding their bike with no hands or making strange and irritating sounds at the dinner table. Sometimes their behavior shocks their parents. Sometimes it pleases them to observe certain skills. Sometimes it annoys them. One thing it always does—it attracts attention. It is a way of trying to get the attention they feel is (and in fact it may be) lacking in their lives.

Often when children are going through divorce, the parent they live with is very busy. He or she is preoccupied with handling finances, dealing with loss, sorting through self-image, regaining confidence, finding housing, dealing with legal proceedings, finding or maintaining employment, arranging child care and so on. Mothers who are not already working outside the home, may have to do so to contribute to the family support. That in turn gives her less time for the children. Further, because the parent at home is working through a major trauma, he or she is less emotionally able to give. The children feel a strong need for attention and may express that need by acting it out. Bravely showing off on the surface may indicate a lack of self-esteem underneath.

On occasion showoffs are expressing inner tension, gaining release by taking action. When children feel the pressure inside and can't understand the feelings, let alone put them into words, they feel like doing something. Increase in the activity level of children may serve as a tension release.

Another reason for showing off is to reestablish one's sense of achievement which may in turn seem to give one more worth. In addition to saying, "Notice me," showoffs can be saying, "Hey, I'm really good at this. I can skate better than anybody on the block. Therefore, I'm worth something." It is a familiar concept among adults to tie your worth to your performance. Yet that concept is not biblical. Jesus taught the multitudes, not just the successful people of his day, that the meek and lowly were the salt of the earth and the light of the world. He taught concepts like "the first shall be last." He said to give to those who cannot repay.

In spite of his teachings, the concept of worth by performance permeates our society. It sheds light on why children try to achieve more self-worth at a point in their life where it may have come into question.

In dealing with showoffs a useful course of action is for significant people in their lives (parents, teachers, grandparents, uncles or aunts) to find ways of giving them attention without rewarding them for inappropriate and sometimes obnoxious behavior. The trick is to meet the need while not responding favorably to the undesirable expression of that need. To learn the value that God places on every person may best be taught children through experiencing it in a tangible human relationship. A loving human being can reflect God's love of the child and his or her value to him by giving attention at a point where the child is feeling a lack of being valued.

Bullies

Bullies begin to give orders to other children. They may boss them around, become domineering with peers and always try to be running the show. They may soon develop the reputation of being mean, physically hitting or lashing out verbally at other children. Bullies tend to see the world as a cold and rejecting place that is treating them harshly, and they in turn begin treating other people harshly. Life centers around the unaccepting world in which they live. Bullies need to be loved and accepted, although they may reject love when it is offered. It does not fit their perception of the world. It is important, however, for the significant people in their lives to continue to love and accept them even though their initial reaction may be akin to resistance.

The harsh world of bullies includes their anger at their parents splitting up and leaving them. Because they are not able to verbalize their feelings, they take them out on other people. Perhaps they feel it is too risky to tell their parents how angry they are. It is less risky to hit a little brother or sister. When they push someone around and as a result find relief from some inner frustration, their relief tends to reinforce that negative behavior. Of course, a secondary gain is that it keeps people at a distance. That means they are less likely to get hurt in the future if people were too close emotionally to them.

Bullies are often boys, who tend to be more aggressive than girls. Bill, at thirteen, was the oldest of four children. He was tall for his age and husky. His parents divorced after fourteen years of marriage. At that time his father gave up the value system he had espoused for years and left the church. Whenever Bill's mom and dad saw each other, there was an immediate loud and harsh fight. In between their meetings, hostility constantly surged through their lives with accusations, insults and court battles. For months their lives centered on their animosity toward one another.

Bill became more and more of a behavior problem to his mother. The younger children in the family often got hurt when he pushed them around. Even when their mother was home, there were fights. Bill became surly and would saunter around the house with a chip on his shoulder, just waiting for someone to cross him or disagree with him. It was a year or more before he began to cool off and slowly adjust to the divorce.

Occasionally the bully is a girl. Julie's mother brought her daughter for counseling because of her temper. She bullied her younger sister and also got into fights at school. After the divorce, Julie had moved back and forth between her parents for a while. She liked living with her dad the best, except for her new stepmother. After a while she felt less and less acceptance from the stepmother as well as from her dad; he felt he needed to support the stepmother. Finally, they sent her to live permanently with her mother. Her world seemed very harsh to her. First, her dad had left, then she wasn't liked by her stepmother, then her dad sent her away and she wasn't so sure about her mom's commitment to her either. Her athletic ability made her a natural for becoming a successful bully. She got recognition and attention for fighting. She became a bully as a way of dealing with the divorce.

Bullies need "tough love." They need to be able to deal with their anger and alter their perception of the world. This means consistent interaction with someone who can set limits, help create a more positive world and yet be open to helping them deal with anger. The biblical assurances of God's goodness and forgiveness will be meaningful when they can experience them through others.

Loners

Loners are children who tend to be scared, self-condemning and shy. At times loners express themselves as feeling worthless, even when people try to convince them otherwise. These children tend to deal with their feelings about the divorce by withdrawing. They appear to accept whatever comes along. Since there is not a lot of unacceptable or wild behavior, and they are not vocal, some may think they are handling the separation well. In the meantime, turmoil is going on inside.

Becoming a loner may be a magnification of a tendency

that was present in the first place. Although many children are shy, a divorce may create true isolation. Often such children don't like being loners and even condemn themselves for being that way. That in turn complicates the vicious circle they are in. Loners may feel that they are victims of unfair circumstances and therefore become passive rather than taking an active role in finding relief. They need to be able to focus on and be involved with others rather than dwelling only on themselves and possibly forming permanent self-concepts as loners. If older, they need to recognize that this is the way they are coping as opposed to being "just the way I am."

Loners can become scapegoats for other children, which complicates the situation. Loners need adults around them to draw them out, not allowing them to be quiet and by themselves all the time. They need to be consistently encouraged to participate in other activities. Sometimes they are helped by an adult inviting them out to a movie or for a pizza on a one-to-one basis. Taking a child to a ball game or to the zoo or something appropriate to the child's interests would be a step toward bringing them out. These should not be one-time events; repeated interactions are needed. Also arrange for loners to be around other children, particularly other children who tend to encourage rather than compete with the loners.

There is a tendency to ignore the quiet child who doesn't ask anything, makes no demands and doesn't need correcting for bouncing all through the house making noise. Yet we want to emphasize that quietness should blare out to adults an emotional need that is going unattended. Often the child has decided that the parents' divorce means that he or she isn't acceptable. These children feel that the best way to deal with unacceptance is to stay by themselves and not get involved. They feel it is best not to open up to others. Here again, the need is great to understand the value God places on everyone, the uniqueness we all have that makes us of special worth. Christ's relationship to Mary and Martha demonstrates his love for two very different personality types in the same family. Their difference did not determine whether he accepted or rejected them.

Clinging Vines

Clinging vines are children who become very dependent. These children may have been quite self-sufficient previously, but now need the significant adult—teacher, mother, relative or someone else—to help them tie their shoes, prepare lessons or help with tasks that before were rather routine. They tend to hang on to the adults. They have need for much physical interaction. If younger, they may want to be held on the adult's lap. They may not want to stay all night at a friend's house and may develop all kinds of good reasons not to attend school. Sometimes they get sick or hurt so that somebody has to be home and take care of them. When the remaining parent is gone longer than expected to the store or out for the evening, they begin to get concerned and repeatedly ask the baby sitter when the parent will return.

These children tend to feel incapable. They lack confidence in their ability to deal with issues. Their world has become insecure because significant people have left. If you want to be sure someone won't leave, you stay with them where you can keep an eye on them. That way you won't be surprised, and besides you may even be able to hang on to them.

When his mother returned after a period of separation, nine-year-old Bud literally followed her everywhere in the house. She felt smothered by his behavior and pulled away more, which served to increase his clinging efforts. He was trying to entwine himself around her to achieve a sense of security. The security that hadn't seemed like a big thing when he had it became a very big thing when he didn't have it.

It is important to allow these children to do tasks at which they can succeed and so help them step-by-step toward self-reliance. They need to discover that they can achieve goals. They need to be given much reassurance of their own ability to take care of themselves (in areas that are realistic).

They need significant adults to help deal with the fear of being abandoned. They need, through interaction with others as well as through verbal assurance, to know what it means to "stick closer than a brother." They need to know experientially what Christ meant when he said, "I will never fail you nor forsake you" (Heb 13:5). Only as their fears begin to be relieved can they begin to let go of their clinging behavior.

Everybody's Friend

The child who is everybody's friend becomes very co-operative and compliant. These children will do anything you want them to do. They even anticipate doing things for you you hadn't even thought of. They are eager to please, yet their feelings are hurt easily if they are not able to accomplish this. They tend to be responsive to both other children and adults. They smile a lot. Their way of coping is to please everybody so that nobody else will reject them. They don't want to create enemies. They tend to believe there is safety in numbers, so, the more friends you have, the better off you are.

They may have felt as though they have been very bad, and therefore created a situation where their parents left each other. Now they are making up for their actions by being very good. Their theory is that if you're good enough, then everyone will accept you and like you and life will be smooth and maybe Mom and Dad will get back together again.

These children need encouragement to realize that they were not rejected because of their bad performance. In fact, they weren't rejected at all. They needed help when disagreeing with other people to know they still can be accepted. All children must begin to be realistic about several factors. First, not everyone is going to like us or be pleased with us. By setting unrealistically high expecta-tions, we are putting ourselves in a bind. It is more realistic to live a life of self-expression, showing concern for others but not always expecting a friendly response nor attempting to elicit a certain response.

Children need to separate their worth from their ability to perform. They need to know that they don't have to earn acceptance from everybody. When we work to earn acceptance, we become slaves of the expectations of others. As long as children are imprisoned in that web, they are unable to be the person God created them to be. They have no sense of freedom, but are constantly expending their energy to say and do what they think pleases others.

The difficulty with the people-pleasing children is that teachers or parents are often delighted with their behavior. They forget to consider that they may be expressing deeper needs.

Organizers
Children who react to divorce by becoming organizers like everything very tidy and in order. These children compartmentalize everything precisely. They want to find right and wrong answers to every question. They feel a need to get everything shipshape and planned out in minute detail. They try to get others to do what they want them to do. They go to great lengths to structure their environment. These children constantly organize their school work, their room and their daily activities. They try to organize the family, especially the more cooperative little brothers and sisters. They like to make lists so they have a complete picture of possible alternatives.

Organizers like to control the world around them for

two reasons. First, they feel that this world which has provided some sense of security is falling apart. Long ago they learned that when you feel insecure you organize your world. That way you re-establish control and thereby keep yourself from harm or emotional hurt. When the parents of such children decided to separate, great risk entered their world, and their organizational response came into play. They may feel as though the old security can be achieved if one simply works hard enough. If such efforts do not cause the reconciliation, they will tend to organize other aspects of life more extensively.

Another reason for all the organization is to prevent any new painful surprises. These children perceive the world as a very unpleasant place, full of terrible shocks unless one really controls it. They deal with the hurt of losing the parent by trying to gain greater influence over their world so that similar experiences will not happen in the future.

Of course, children need to be allowed to develop structure in their lives. At the same time they should be learning to relax their defenses by having consistent, dependable interaction with people who are accepting of them. They need to experience the support of significant people so they learn that although life is difficult, painful situations need not overwhelm them. With support, children can grow through these hard experiences. When we can see value in difficult experiences, it changes both our interpretation of the experience and our need to try and ward it off through organization. The apostle Paul says in Philippians 4 that he knew how to be in need and in a position of no need. Either way he had learned to be content because of the strength the Lord had given him.

Can we really trust that God is not going to dish out more than we can deal with? Can we grow to accept as his will and direction the steps he has ordered for us? Do we really know there will be sufficient grace for every need? At the heart of this issue is the question of whether or not God is good. With his goodness as a foundation on which to interpret our experiences, we have less need to try to control our world. Of course this sense of God being good makes more sense to small children when they experience the goodness of their parents and other significant adults.

Grouches

Grouches are not really pleased by any expenence. These children get upset when any little thing goes wrong and are quite distressed by any minor change in their environment. They are easily irritated and constantly complain about one thing or another not being right. They drive their parents to distraction by their constant whining. At times they become listless. They play with friends but don't really seem to enjoy anything that happens. They never seem satisfied, no matter what good experiences come across their path. These children have symptoms of a childhood depression; they simply cannot seem to receive any fulfillment or enjoyment out of life, regardless of the circumstances.

Grouches need to be able to deal with their hurt and angry feelings in a more direct way. They need loving limits within which they can be accepted and still be angry. They need love and assurance to deal with their anger appropriately. One difficulty with this particular dynamic is that often parents end up being frustrated with them which only contributes further to their not adjusting to the new situation. The children draw the parents into a pattern of interacting with them, but much of the interaction is negative rather than supportive. The children may well have a lot of repressed anger toward the parent who left but feel incapable of getting it out. Often younger children cannot even identify the feeling. They just know that life is miserable. For older children this is an area they need to focus on, discussing with a more mature person how to handle their angry feelings.

Margo's parents decided to get a divorce when she was two and a half. Although her father had moved out, he tried to spend time with her at least twice a week. After these visits she was easily distressed, whined and complained constantly. When not getting her way, she would not argue back, but acted restless and resisted suggestions and requests. She was short-tempered and would snap at other children she played with. Margo would moan whenever she was asked to share a toy or to eat her vegetables. Frequently she would cry, but was hard pressed to produce real tears. The crying could be turned off in the blink of an eye when she chose. For her, hope for the future came through months of loving structure offered by a woman who baby-sat her while her mother worked outside the home. She needed to be able to deal with her frustration about her parents. Over time, Margo's sense of acceptance grew. She complained less and became less agitated, more responsive and more enjoyably involved in life.

Little Adults

Little adults accept everything in a mature manner. They do not show a lot of emotion about the divorce or separation; rather, they become very adultlike, almost paternal or maternal. They want, at times, to be able to handle anything Mom can't or their teacher can't or that is a problem for Dad. They readily show everyone that they can take care of anything that comes their way.

They become hyperresponsible around the house, making sure things get done like taking the trash out, getting the room picked up or the dishes done. They may give advice to Mom and express interest in her well-being. They suddenly have learned a lot about a wide variety of adult matters and freely express it.

These children are saying through their behavior, "See, we really don't need Dad around here anyhow; we can make it without him." That reassurance is a veneer. These children are trying their best to deny that any major loss has occurred. The reality is that a major loss has occurred, and there should be feelings of loss and grief.

These children are trying to regain the missing parent by replacing them. Their behavior is a form of trying to adapt to the loss of someone who was very important.

These children should not receive a lot of praise for this behavior, which is what often happens. They need a chance to be a child. They need the opportunity not to have a lot of responsibility nor to have to be mature so they can deal with their feelings about the parent actually being gone. They need to realize they don't have to replace them. Expressing their emotional dependency and loss is an important need. Childhood needs to be left intact for the maturation process to take place at a reasonable pace. Only as this maturation is left in place can adulthood develop in a consistent pattern. To tell a child that he is now the man in the family tends to foster problems that will surface at some future point.

The support of another person who may fill some of those needs for dependence can be helpful. Of course, if it is Dad who left, his consistent attention is the most useful of all.

These are just a few of the most common ways children react to divorce. As we said earlier, many children will exhibit a combination of patterns. But viewing the world from their perspective can be the beginning of meeting their needs.

The Absent Parent and Special Circumstances

> *Children have never been very good at listening to their elders, but they have never failed to imitate them.*
> —James Baldwin

5

After divorce it is common for routines to be set up so that the parent who has moved out can keep in contact with the children. The child or children are somehow shuttled back and forth between the two homes. This chapter deals with some problems that arise under those circumstances.

A Realistic Environment

When Jane's parents separated, it was decided that Jane would see her father every other weekend. During those weekends, she and her father played lots of games, went to amusement parks, had picnics, ate out most of the time at fast-food restaurants and went on day-trips to the mountains or beach. Her father would buy her lots of things: a new bike, new dresses and play clothes, table games and toys. Needless to say, Jane enjoyed her time with her father. When she got home, she quickly became irritated that her mother would not spend similarly large quantities of time with her and buy her other things she wanted.

Also, being a typical child, Jane disliked doing chores around the home. And there was always work to do: making her bed, feeding the dog, washing dishes, emptying wastebaskets, raking leaves, cleaning her room. At her father's apartment, most of the chores were already out of the way and completed by the time she arrived. Since he was free from child care and family responsibilities in the evenings and had spare time, he was able to keep up with those chores himself.

Further, her father never seemed to discipline her, whereas her mother was continually scolding her for one thing or another. As a consequence, Jane began to rebel against her mother and told her that she loved her father more.

Parents who do not normally live with the children tend to avoid exposing them to a realistic home environment. Such parents usually have time between visits to fulfill their personal social commitments. They are not burdened with the day-in, day-out problems of child rearing: getting the kids ready for bed, having them take baths, solving sibling quarrels, making sure they're doing homework instead of watching TV and so on. Hence, absent parents have time and emotional energy to spend on the children during the relatively few days they see them. Often absent parents feel guilty about the divorce and try to make up for it on these weekends.

Parents who see their children on a limited basis can do a number of things to provide a realistic relationship. First, they can schedule some of the day-to-day routines for the weekend and avoid entertaining their children with a continuous stream of exciting events. The children might be given the responsibility of completing a number of chores around the home during the time they are there. This will help them to understand that things are not all fun there either. Such responsibilities might be to dust, empty wastepaper baskets or vacuum the carpet. However, cleaning a week's worth of dirty dishes or the parent's clutter from the past week is not a good idea.

Time might also be spent going to the supermarket, laundromat or auto-repair shop. Children don't have to expect every day to be a fun day with the parent they don't live with. Sharing normal daily experiences is a basis for growth in the parent-child relationship. Staying at home together and helping with homework, reading interesting books, drawing pictures or playing games can bring parent and child close. These can be times of helping the child build new skills, like helping Dad change the oil in the car or helping Mom fix a broken toy.

Second, parents need to avoid giving children an overabundance of presents and treats, just as they would if the child were living in an intact family where both parents were seen daily. Many parents are tempted to provide lots of *things* for their children forgetting that quality *time* spent together is the most valuable gift a parent can give. Children will always want various items; parents must not give in to such wishes as a means of gaining their favor. In the long run, and possibly even in the short run, children will be most glad for the quality time they received.

The desire to shower children with gifts also tempts the parent who usually lives with the children. The pain they are feeling is seen by that parent who wants somehow to make their world all right again. It is better, however, to focus on growth through the situation rather than over-compensating for it.

Third, guidelines and rules need to be set for the visiting children. Many parents make the mistake of giving their children great freedom during the visit. On the other hand, it is in the children's best interest to have structure similar to what they have at home (assuming that such structure exists—which is not always the case). These rules could be a specified bedtime, taking a bath each evening, eating all the food on one's plate, a limitation on how much TV can be watched. By making sure that certain standards apply on weekends, a parent can instill a sense of continuity into the child's life. Two divergent lifestyles and discipline systems are inevitable in two households, yet some form of consistency can also become a pattern that provides security.

Time with the Child

Becky's parents divorced when she was four years old. Her mother received custody. At that time her father made many promises: to take her to ball games, spend summers together and go on fishing and camping trips. Later, numerous "good reasons" were given as to why things needed to be cancelled, but somehow all those trips never happened, and Becky rarely saw her father.

At the age of seven, Becky was referred to a counselor because of her behavior. She was becoming increasingly unmanageable at school. She spoke of hating and wanting to kill people around her. Finally she began talking about killing herself.

In therapy it was discovered that Becky harbored a lot of resentment toward her father. That resentment became magnified when her father remarried and mentioned the possibility of having a baby with his new wife. It was bad enough knowing that her father didn't want to spend time with her. It was worse knowing that he spent a lot of time with his new wife. But Becky did not seem able to control her emotions when she found out that another child was going to move into the picture and possibly receive the attention she was lacking. The pain that Becky experienced could have been avoided to a great degree had her father made conscious efforts to spend significant periods of time with her.

Children pay a high price when a parent is removed from the family network. A recent study that focused on the effects of father-absence found a number of patterns.

These were not universal sets of behavior, but statistical tendencies:

☐ Young boys who were raised apart from their fathers had increased chances of developing inappropriate sex-role behaviors. Because they lacked a male model in their home, they had difficulty determining what an appropriate masculine role was.

☐ Boys raised without their father tended to have a lower level of moral development when compared to boys raised in families where the father was present.

☐ Girls raised in father-absent families had greater tendencies to behave inappropriately in heterosexual relationships. Because many had been unable to obtain love and affection from their fathers, they later attempted to seek fulfillment of that need from male peer relationships.

☐ Both boys and girls raised apart from their fathers tended to exhibit lower academic performance than those raised with their fathers.[1]

It is important that children and the parents who have left home have a continuing strong relationship. Sometimes either the parent with the child or the other parent moves a long distance away, as is common among professional people. In such a case frequent letters and phone calls can help fill in the gaps between visits.

Parents who leave often follow a pattern that needs to be guarded against. During the first two months after separation, they typically see the children frequently and sometimes spend more time with them than prior to the separation. After several months they get more involved in their work and in seeking new relationships, and their contacts with their children begin to decline. Gradually, over the next two years, there comes a marked decrease in both the quality and quantity of parent-child relationships.[2] Frequently this pattern is related to the father's feelings of having failed in something important. Such parents then strive to meet their needs through work and meeting others and in the process underestimate their children's needs.

The Other Parent

Twelve-year-old Janet was shuttled back and forth between her parents. During her stay with each of them, she had to put up with their repeated abusive statements about each other. Janet's mother continually berated her father: he did not seem to be able to hold down a steady job, he broke promises to Janet about seeing her, he was often late picking her up, he used foul language around her. Janet's father spoke to her about her mother's undesirable boyfriends, her sloppy housekeeping, her drinking problem, her overall ineffectiveness as a mother.

Janet's parents did not realize how much stress this caused their daughter. She wanted to love each of her parents, but found it difficult when continually exposed to all the negative attributes of each.

To make themselves look good to their child and to gain an ally for support, many parents attempt to lower their children's opinion of the other parent. This often

serves as a release for their own hostility as well. Obviously, it is better for the welfare of the child for a parent to
gain favor by engaging in positive behavior.

What about the parent who really does behave in an
undesirable way? Is it possible to help children see that
such conduct is not good without alienating them from
the other parent? A mother could, for example, tell her
children that their father is a "no-good drunk who couldn't
care less about them." A better way to communicate that,
and one that would give the child a more accurate perception of the situation, might be to say, "Your father has
a drinking problem, and because he is drunk much of the
time he doesn't think of how much you would like to be
with him." It is important for parents to communicate to
children that although they are dissatisfied with certain
aspects of the other parent's behavior, that parent has
positive qualities for which he or she can be admired and
valued.

Questions, Questions

When Sharon was picked up each Friday afternoon by
her father he would immediately question her about what
was going on at home. He wanted to know what time she
went to bed at night, how much work she did around the
house, how often she and her mother ate out, whether
her mother ever left her alone at night without a sitter,
how she was doing in school, whether her mother had a
boyfriend and so on. Sharon understood that her father
was asking those questions because he didn't think her

mother was doing a good job with her. Similarly, when she returned from weekend visits with her father, her mother always wanted to know the details of what went on during the weekend visit, taking special interest in events she disapproved of.

All that questioning was hard on Sharon. Both parents expected her to be on their side and "spill the beans" on the other. Sharon felt increasingly uncomfortable with the dual allegiance that was expected of her.

It is proper for parents to want to find out what is happening in their child's life. Most parents would want to know if their child received a special award at school, lost their first tooth, wrote a poem about a butterfly, caught three trout on a fishing trip or built a model airplane. There is, of course, nothing wrong in asking children to tell you about the interesting things that are happening in their life. Children love to tell their parents those things. Problems arise when children are asked probing questions that seek to discover undesirable situations in the home.

Rather than attempting to obtain answers to difficult questions about the child's life and the other parent's life from the child, parents could try to obtain those answers directly from the other parent. Let that parent know you would like to work out a way to communicate with each other rather than through the child. That can be difficult to bring about with some divorced parents, but it is certainly more desirable than putting children through those uncomfortable periods of questioning where they feel they are disappointing one parent if they don't tell and are betraying the other parent if they do.

No-Show Parent

What does one do about the absent parent who seldom or never shows up to see the children? Bill promises that he is going to pick up his children on Saturday mornings and keep them for the weekend. Saturday morning the children get ready and look forward to the time with Father with anticipation and excitement. At 9:00 A.M., when he is due to arrive, he does not show up. They wait patiently until 9:30 and then begin looking out the window. Bill still does not show. Eventually the children resolve the situation by going off to play.

These children need to receive support and encouragement in special ways from the parent they are living with. Their mother should deal realistically with the circumstance. She might explain that one of the areas their father struggles with is to be consistent with what he says he is going to do. The tendency is strong in children to feel that the father doesn't show because they are undeserving. The remaining parent needs to minimize the impact of the disappointment by providing reassurance in that area. It is not useful for the mother or father to berate the other, walk around the house bombarding the children with their own anger or tear down the other's character. Neither is it useful for them to make excuses for the parent, such as, "Well, Bill probably isn't here because the car broke down," when this problem has occurred three Saturdays in a row.

When the absent parent consistently misses, it is best to help the children think realistically about the "promised" outings. It may at times be difficult, since they may cling to the hope that their father will come for sure the next time. Whenever the father sets plans, some realistic deciphering of the situation could go like this:

Child Dad promised to pick me up Saturday to go to the ball game.

Mother That certainly sounds exciting, but I wonder what that promise really means. For some people, telling someone you will pick them up at noon means you will arrive at noon and pick them up. For others, they mean it is something that seems good to them but they probably won't really do it.

Child No, Dad said we are going to the game.

Mother Well, I hope it works out because it sounds like something you'd really like to do. But remember, he hasn't shown up the last three times he promised to do that. So his saying he wants to take you to the ball game might mean something else to him.

In that exchange, the mother keeps presenting reality to the child without assaulting the father's character. Berating the father would probably only make the child defensive.

Sometimes parents who divorce make all kinds of unrealistic promises to children about taking them away on extended vacations or buying them a horse or moving to a ranch. When such statements are made, the most useful thing is for the other parent to provide at least some questioning about the difference between having hopes, dreams and plans and what will probably happen.

The Physically Violent Parent

Occasionally one parent persists in physical violence toward the parent with whom the child is living. Usually in those circumstances, physical violence was present for some time previous to the divorce or separation; often it was part of the dynamic that caused the decision to separate or divorce. Children need to be protected from that type of interaction between two people they love. If the parents cannot refrain from fighting, care needs to be taken to avoid their meeting even when picking up or dropping off the children. In extreme cases a restraining order can be legally drawn, which prohibits this type of abuse.

Dating Again

After a period of time following the divorce and in some cases prior to the divorce being final, it is common to find one or both parents dating again. Younger children may see that as a threat to their own needs for attention and therefore resent the new person immediately. Most children regard the newcomer as interfering with their dream that Mom and Dad will reunite and, therefore, complain about the relationship. Other children, however, will seek out the new person and show off or cling to him or her to fulfill an emotional need that the absent parent is not meeting.

Where an older boy has been in a responsible role in the family, he may feel threatened that he will be pushed out of that role. Other times older children will be pleased that Mom is dating again. They have been concerned about her well-being and think that this will make her happy again. Sometimes, with older adolescent girls, dating becomes an area of competition with their mother which creates new tension.

With Dad's dating, the issue is complicated when the woman friend is part of the reason he left in the first place. The older children may harbor much resentment if they believe she caused the separation.

The main issue with children is to use good sense when with the date and the children. Children should be introduced and have the opportunity to meet this new person, especially if the parent has more than a passing interest. Children need the opportunity to talk to their parent about what this individual means to their own lives. They need to discuss their feelings, both positive and negative. Parents need to be wise in balancing their own needs for companionship against the emotional needs of their children. If parents are going through a lot of turmoil about a relationship, children should be protected from that stress. Mom should not be saying that Bill will possibly be their new stepfather and the following month say the same thing about Jim.

We encourage parents to focus on their adjustment and their children's adjustment and not involve themselves in any serious commitments until at least one year after their divorce. Both children and parents need time to work through emotional issues to establish a firm basis from which to build new relationships.

Adolescence

*So much of adolescence is an
ill-defined dying,
An intolerable waiting,
A longing for another place
and time,
Another condition.*
—Theodore Roethke

6

Adolescents are at an entirely different developmental stage from younger children. Yet those in high school and entering their college years still experience many things intensely, including their parents' divorce.

Divorce during Adolescence

The need to depend primarily on parents for support, love and nurture is characteristic of children. Adolescents, however, have realized much of their intellectual, emotional and physical growth and are beginning to become more independent from their parents.

Unlike younger children who may be angry yet fear

expressing it, adolescents are more independent and are therefore safer in being openly hostile. Hostility becomes a tool for pushing their way out of the home. A divorce can force adolescents to change their speed of growth toward independence and adulthood.

This pressure can cause one of several reactions. Adolescents who feel overburdened by great demands, fears, expectations and anxiety may slow in their development. They may stay dependent and attach themselves to one parent. On the other hand, the calamity of a divorce may spur adolescents to early maturity and independence. They may quickly focus their attention outside the home and become virtually uninvolved with either parent.[1]

Changed perception of parents. Fifteen-year-old Jane had always looked favorably on her mother and father prior to their divorce. She knew they fought about financial matters and had few common interests, but still she saw each of them in a positive light. During the divorce, however, Jane saw a different side of her mother and father. After her father moved out of the house, her mother changed from her usually confident and secure self to an insecure, weak individual with low self-esteem. She depended on Jane to help her make a majority of decisions about her side of the divorce. When she did make her own decisions they often seemed irrational to Jane.

Because of the free lifestyle her father was living, Jane saw him as being rather self-centered. He had always encouraged her to stick to a job or project until she saw it turn out right—and now she saw him as one who was unwilling to work out his own problems with her mother. In her eyes her father was not the person of moral integrity that he once was. Her idealized image of her parents came crashing down, rather than slowly changing as her awareness and maturity grew naturally.

Divorce forces adolescents to see their parents as individuals. That awareness tends to diminish their sense of security at a time when comfort and security are needed while they test their own wings. Likewise, the painful loss of the ideal parent may affect their own self-worth if they have identified closely with that parent.

Adolescents need to feel the freedom to make their own assessments of their parents' behavior. They are at an age where they are able to make cognitive judgments of what behavior is appropriate and not appropriate, desirable and undesirable. While it can be painful, there are advantages for adolescents to see their parents as individuals. First, it helps them accept personality differences in people, realizing that everyone has inherent strengths and weaknesses. That can help them come to terms with the divorce. They can understand that a divorce has occurred not between two ideal and integrated parents, but between two dynamic and changing individuals. Second, understanding that their mother and father are distinct individuals frees adolescents to pursue their own identity. They no longer feel compelled to conform to predetermined standards but may now construct a separate identity apart from their parents. It is hoped that their new identity would include the knowledge that not knowing themselves well could cause difficulties in their own future relationships.

Competition. Following a divorce, most parents will begin socializing. Some will seek out friends of their own sex to build a network of people they can spend time with and gain support from. Others will, in addition, re-enter the dating scene to fulfill their heterosexual companionship needs.

While the former behavior is acceptable to most adolescents, the latter often causes a great concern. Adolescent dating years are times of emotional growth, increased understanding of the opposite sex and increased self-awareness. Adolescents often feel deprived of their dating parent's full interest during that phase, interest they would normally receive from parents already content in a long-established marriage.

Divorced fathers often begin dating women who are much younger than they are. When their dating partners begin to approach the age of a parent's sons or daughters, adolescents are often angry and jealous.

Vicky was sixteen years old when her parents divorced. Although she spent most of her time living at her mother's house she saw her father a couple of times a month. A year after the divorce, Vicky's father began dating a twenty-one-year-old he knew from where he worked. Vicky was not bothered too much at first; her father should be able to do what he wanted, she thought. Then one Saturday she met her father's friend. She was shocked and surprised at how close she was to her own age. The young woman looked as though she could have been her older sister. Vicky became jealous that her father spent a lot of time with this young woman both during the week and on weekends. She also felt increasingly uncomfortable with her dad. She began to develop a new awareness of him as a sexual being, a feeling that might not have arisen had it not been for his girlfriend's being so close to her own age.

Parents need to be aware of how their social behavior can affect adolescent children. Fathers sometimes date much younger woman to reassure their bruised egos of their own attractiveness to the opposite sex. That may require time to work through their feelings about themselves, especially if they are experiencing a midlife crisis in conjunction with the divorce.

As parents begin to date, sometimes they dress and act younger than they are. Mothers often change their hairstyle to a younger look, change their hemlines to the current fashion and adopt some of the behaviors characteristic of the younger set. Competition can develop with a college-age daughter who dresses in a similar fashion. It is understandable for parents to want to be in style and be attractive, but that desire needs to be tempered to an appropriate age level. Sometimes the tendency to become more adolescentlike is part of a wider issue of regression, for which parents should seek professional counseling.

Troubled future. We all have a tendency to project our present plight or calamity into the future. Adolescents are no different. Adolescents from divorced families worry about two main areas: lack of financial support, and the feeling that possibly they will never or should never marry.

Adolescents who intend to go to college seem most concerned over the family's disrupted economic state. They realize that educational costs can be difficult to meet and many begin worrying a lot. Those feelings often seem to change, though, as they become accustomed to the restructured family. Although struggles will continue, these adolescents see new opportunities develop that they never envisioned before. These both take time, but both can lessen worry.

Because they have seen firsthand the difficulties, struggles and pains of marriage, many adolescents decide they don't want to run the risk of getting married. They may also feel puzzled or confused since their ideas of marriage have suddenly changed. The decision not to marry is usually made around the time of the divorce, when tempers are hot, accusations are flying, cooperation is lacking and at least one parent is scarce at home.

A recent study showed that adolescents who made a decision not to marry after their parents divorced usually had a change of heart a year later.[2] Time is usually needed to rethink such a decision. The acute pain experienced toward the end of the divorce needs to subside before adolescents can feel good about the enjoyable times that the family had together in previous years.

Many adolescents will also become more aware of how other adults are successfully living out their married lives and providing positive models. Such couples convey that there are struggles in marriage, but that those struggles can be balanced through loving times of giving, sharing and sacrificing by both partners. Trying to argue adolescents out of a decision to never marry rarely helps. They need time to heal. Besides, their decision not to marry may be the right one for them.

Guilt feelings. There is a tendency for parents to remain together and struggle through difficult times for the sake of their children. Tracy's parents did that until she and her two older sisters were out of the nest. Soon after Tracy left home to attend an out-of-state college her parents filed for divorce. Tracy was devastated; she felt a heavy responsibility for the breakup, believing that the divorce would not have occurred if she had stayed home to attend a local college. She was probably correct about the effects of her leaving. For years she had filled the unhealthy role of a buffer between her parents. But she was not correct about being responsible for her parents' decision to divorce.

Yet sensitive adolescents will heap blame on themselves and experience such guilt feelings about their parents' divorce. There seems to be little difference between the guilt experienced by children and adolescents. Adolescents will often try to get rid of those feelings through attempts to reunite their parents.

Fifteen-year-old Mike said he had conscious reasons for his behavior after he learned of his parents' intentions to divorce. He began to run away from home for short periods of time. After a few days, he would call his parents so they could come and pick him up. He was always pleased to see them come together with mutual concern over his well-being. As the oldest of six siblings, he felt that it was his responsibility to hold them together, and this was one way he knew he could do it. Adolescents need much reassurance about the parents' responsibility as individuals for terminating their own marriage.

Keeping their distance. Many adolescents will stay away as much as possible from the family environment during and after a divorce. Adolescents are already inclined to remove themselves bit by bit from their parents' domain. Many times a divorce intensifies that inclination.

Adolescents affected by divorce may spend more and more time at their friends' homes, at church functions or just hanging out away from home. In this way they avoid the pain that divorce brings on and reduce their anxiety.

This response can be particularly difficult for the dependent parent. Many will want what is left of their broken family to pull together and become closer. They have a difficult time understanding their adolescent's needs just as the adolescent often fails to realize the immediate needs of the dependent parent. Yet those who keep their distance from parent conflicts seem to adapt fastest and best.

Surrogate parent. Debby's parents divorced when she was thirteen years old. The courts gave custody of her and her younger brother and sister to Debby's mother. During the ensuing years, Debby's mother left more and more of the parenting and basic household duties up to Debby while she assumed the responsibilities of providing an income for the family. By the time Debby was eighteen, she had grown tired of that role. She dealt with the stress by getting out of the home. Soon she married a new boyfriend she had known for only a few months.

Adolescents are often called on to fulfill a vacated parental niche in the family, a difficult position for them. They have their own adolescent growth to contend with (which is confusing at best), as well as a new demanding adult role of parenting. Parents should avoid using adolescents as assistant parents and allow them to grow up at a normal pace.

Loyalty conflict. Jim was a kind and sensitive adolescent who deeply cared for his parents. Largely because of his ability to listen and show concern for each parent's position, Jim often found himself hearing his mother's and father's sides of the story. It wasn't long before he began to feel the tension of being the confidant of each parent. He felt pressure to side with the particular parent he was speaking to at the time. When his mother and father began to ask him difficult questions about the other parent, Jim began to lie to put each parent in a good light. He wanted to keep peace between them, even if it meant compromising his honesty. Parents may often come to adolescents for advice, support and empathy concerning the divorce. When both parents confide in and seek comfort from the adolescent, a loyalty conflict arises, a problem of dual allegiance. It is always best to avoid using adolescents or children for this purpose. While parents need the support and reassurance of loved ones, they should seek that support from other family members and friends.

Telling friends. Even though divorce is becoming commonplace in our society, a certain degree of anxiety and embarrassment still exists about telling one's peers. It is hard to confess that your mom and dad had problems they were not able to overcome. Many adolescents have difficulty not thinking that the divorce must also be a reflection on their own character and ability to function.

Changes of any kind are almost always difficult. God, however, has created us with the ability to be resilient, to bounce back. Although it takes time, we usually adjust to new situations. That is true with divorce. The trauma of learning about the divorce will begin to diminish in later months. That fact is not usually evident to adolescents, but they do struggle through it. Their tendency to live in the present makes it difficult to understand how they will feel adjusted to the divorce in a few years.

Looking Back on the Divorce

A second aspect of adjustment concerns adolescents whose parents divorced when they were children. Now in their teens they begin to rethink the divorce and to deal with several issues.

Role model. As adolescents begin to see themselves being married, examples play an important part in their thinking. What is it like to be a wife or husband? How do you handle disagreements? How does a father relate to kids? How do you keep your love for each other alive and growing? The answers to many of these questions are based on how they have seen other couples relate, especially their parents. The answer may thus depend on who raised the adolescent and whether or not the mother or father remarried.

An adolescent boy who had virtually no father to observe may not have much sense of a husband-wife relationship. But an adolescent boy whose mother remarried once or even twice may have to sort out which model makes the most sense.

With a girl the issues may be the same. But often girls have much clearer ideas of what it means to be a woman, even though the husband-wife relationship may be unclear. If their father left while they were young, adolescent girls sometimes have the added pressure of strongly wanting the love of a man. Studies indicate that these girls have a tendency to become more seductive as adolescents in an effort to attract men's attention.[3] Thus there is a great advantage in a family having trustworthy friends of the opposite sex with whom the children spend time. Time with couples who have a good relationship can help too.

Rethinking the other parent. Late adolescents often begin reassessing the parent who did not raise them. That assessment may go in one of two directions. They may have been routinely sent off every other weekend to be with Dad or Mom but don't really feel much rapport or desire to be with him or her. Now that they are older and more mobile they may decide they don't want to keep on doing that, so they begin terminating the weekend visits.

Another shift in how they perceive the absent parent can occur as adulthood approaches. Such a shift can be positive, but it also can create new tensions. Such adolescents begin to view people relative to their strengths and weaknesses rather than as being all good or all bad. Perhaps their mother viewed their father as a terrible person. Late adolescents begin to see some of the subtle ways Mom's feelings have affected her view. Maybe Dad wasn't totally at fault for leaving them, the way Mom always implied. Adolescents may now gain some understanding of the other parent's point of view. Perhaps the father had poured almost all his energy into his job, the mother became exhausted with home responsibility, their romance gradually waned, and neither was able to meet the other's emotional expectations any longer. Adolescents, beginning to see those two sides of the problem, may now be able to forgive their parents.

Sometimes that kind of reassessment can open relationships with parents that have been closed off for years. It is common for late adolescents who have not seen their other parent for years to want to see them. That, however, can cause strain and tension with the parent who has raised them, who can't understand their new desire to see the other parent. One woman mentioned that when she went to visit her estranged father, her mother went on a drinking binge that lasted three weeks. Those tensions need to be openly discussed and dealt with when they surface.[4]

Pushing out—holding on. Adolescents raised by a single parent may find their usual developmental pattern altered. As they begin to assert themselves, express ideas different from the parents', desire more control of their lives and become more demanding, the parents react.

Some single parents feel their children are out of control. They can't wait until the children are eighteen and can leave for an apartment or college. Then their hassles over misbehavior in school and over all their fights will end. Such parents both subtly and openly begin pushing their adolescents out. The last resort for some is to send their children to live with the other parent.

Other single parents have grown close to their adolescents. Their need, however, is to let go rather than hold on to their children. Those who are held on to will resent it and possibly tear away, or else they will acquiesce and end up taking care of the "victimized" parent for life. At age forty they are still at home, more emotionally bound than ever and having difficulty making any life of their own.

Single parents who struggle with pushing out or holding on need friends who can help them gain perspective on their relationship with the adolescent. Someone may need to help mediate the relationship of the pushing-out parent. The holding-on parent needs the consistent support of others as well, so they can let go.

Helping Teachers Help Children

> *Perhaps a child who is fussed over gets a feeling of destiny; he thinks he is in the world for something important and it gives him drive and confidence.*
> —Benjamin Spock

7

Elementary-school teachers spend twenty to twenty-five hours a week in direct contact with students. Although much of this contact focuses on acquiring and developing scholastic abilities, teachers can also help children work through problems in their lives. Sunday-school teachers, too, though limited in the time they spend with students, can help children whose families are in discord.

Some children will openly share their problems with teachers. Others will not. Teachers might learn of a family's difficulties through other students, from the child's parents or relatives, from the child's changed behavior, or from changes in academic performance. An observant teacher can recognize maladaptive symptoms and give support to the child. Though we encourage teachers to read this entire book, this chapter will focus on what can be done in a classroom setting to help children cope with divorce.

Meeting Immediate Needs

Children of divorce need a caring, interested adult who will listen to them. Knowing that divorce is imminent or under way will precipitate a crisis of varying intensity and duration for nearly every child.

In one study, nursery-school teachers reported that children whose parents had divorced within the last year were more likely to want physical contact, had more difficulty getting along in a group and had lower self-esteem.[1]

Such symptoms, however, may not be found in older children, even if they are suffering intensely from internal stress. In one study of children of divorce, ages seven to ten, only about half reflected acute behavior shifts at school. The half who did have symptoms at school became irritable and moody; their grades dropped and they experienced more difficulty relating to peers.[2] Another study found 62 per cent had school behavior problems. Some became aggressive, some possessive. Others were sad and gloomy, with a tendency to give up easily. The other groups became aimless and cried easily.[3]

Art work often indicates these changes. Some teenagers become more active and increase their activities and school performances. Others become less involved, start failing in their classes, have ideas about dropping out of school, and are more angry, intolerant and depressed. Their behavior often shows an attempt to run away from their problems and pain.

People don't necessarily need advice when they are experiencing stress; they do, however, need to talk and get things out in the open to feel better. To listen is the major function in crisis intervention. A teacher can help a student confront a divorce crisis by discussing both the situation and the child's own feelings about it.

One of Miss Smith's students was a usually happy, gregarious seven-year-old boy named Bob. Bob's school performance was above average. His social involvement with his classmates was typical of other children in the class. About two weeks ago, Miss Smith began to notice a change in Bob's behavior. He was beginning to act silly in the classroom, talk incessantly and took part in a number of classroom skirmishes with a few other boys. The quality and quantity of his schoolwork began to go downhill; he was getting low marks on tests, and what little homework he turned in was not up to his usual standards. Miss Smith was tipped off about the source of this problem when she heard Bob mention to a classmate that his dad wasn't living at home. She decided to ask Bob if he would like to stay and have lunch with her that day, thinking that this would give her uninterrupted time to give him an opportunity to talk.

When lunch time came, Miss Smith asked Bob to eat with her. Bob agreed and she sat down in his desk area.

After a short talk about the activities that morning, Miss Smith said, "Bob, I heard you tell Jim that your dad isn't living with you anymore; I bet that makes you feel a lot of things." Bob didn't say anything, but Miss Smith knew she had hit a sensitive area. "What do you feel most, Bob — mad, sad, glad, afraid?"

"I feel afraid," responded Bob.

"What are you afraid of?" asked Miss Smith.

"That my dad may not come back," he replied.

And so it went, as Miss Smith gently encouraged Bob to talk about his feelings concerning his parents' divorce.

A number of things should be kept in mind when talking with children about family discord:

First, let them know you are willing to talk with them about their struggle. Many children are not certain whether they ought to share their home problems with their teacher. A teacher can open up these lines of communication by letting hurting children know that he or she is concerned about their problems at home and is open to talking with them.[4]

Second, tell them you are a good listener—and be one. This is the child's time to do most of the talking. To talk is what will help most.

Third, ask "feeling" questions. Allow the display of feelings. Communicate that it is okay to have strong feelings, that they are natural.

Fourth, be empathetic. Try to feel what the child is feeling by looking at the child's world from his or her frame of reference.

Finally, don't try to become the child's therapist. Family disruption resulting in divorce produces continuing obstacles. It may be appropriate to recommend to parents that the child see a professional therapist.

Self-Esteem

Ideally a teacher should help each child develop good feelings about himself or herself. At times, however, a teacher will be called to work extensively with children who are experiencing acute difficulties with their feelings about themselves. Because children of divorce are often living in homes where their feelings of worth and importance are continually being drained, it is important that significant adult figures in the children's lives attempt to help reverse those feelings. By structuring certain classroom activities, a teacher is able to help these children realize a greater sense of importance and increased self-esteem.

A teacher can help a child realize greater self-esteem in a number of ways:

First, help the child to succeed. While children are experiencing turbulent home lives, it is important that they be successful at school. Give them tasks you are confident they can accomplish that will give them positive feelings about themselves. Find some area that the individual child is good in and provide opportunities for him or her to excel. Depending on the children's abilities and interest, you might have them work on a creative project, read a short book of their choice or let them tell the class about something they have done.

Second, point out talents, abilities and positive characteristics. Make a special effort to help children of divorce become aware of their specific important and unique talents. As we go through life, we usually become accustomed to having people tell us what we don't do well rather than what we do well. A personal compliment is music to the soul and stays with us a long time. Let children know if they have really improved since the beginning of the year in math or spelling, that you really like the way they can kick the ball or the way they look right into your eyes when you talk to them. Granted, this is more difficult with some children than others, but God has made each of us in his image. We are each special in his eyes. Try to recognize special qualities in children and make sure you communicate them.

Third, give recognition. Why does a child feel so good when asked to be window monitor, door monitor, office runner or chalkboard cleaner? Because he or she is being recognized. People thrive on recognition, and children are no different. Give the struggling child the honor of being team captain during recess, let her be in charge of the balls during the play period, allow him to read one of his papers in front of the class, let her show one of her art projects to one of the other classrooms. This is also a positive way to channel excess emotional energy, thus avoiding a multitude of discipline problems. Be careful, though, not to go overboard and make any one child a privileged character.

Fourth, stay on good terms. It is easy for a child's relationship with teachers to take a precipitous downturn when the child's family is in turmoil. It is helpful for the teacher to recognize the source of difficulties and call as little attention as possible to undesirable behavior. By trying to ignore it, and praising positive behavior, a teacher can help shape a child's activities and thus create a desirable interface between teacher and student. Because children often receive little support at home when the parents are in conflict, good rapport with the teacher, as an adult figure, can be a great source of comfort for the distressed child.

Finally, encourage peer-group activities. Children of divorce need to experience positive social interaction with peers. Many tend to become reclusive during difficult family changes, motivated primarily by insecurity. Be on the lookout for children standing alone and encourage them to join peer-group activities. Children feel better about themselves and have a more hopeful outlook on the future if they are discouraged from continually dwelling on family difficulties.

Teachers who are aware of needs, make themselves available and use good relational principles can have a marked effect on children experiencing divorce. Their efforts in this time of crisis can enhance the way the children live out the rest of their lives.

A Story for Children and Parents

*It is not enough
for parents to understand
children. They must
accord children the privilege
of understanding them.*
—Milton R. Sapirstein

8

This chapter is a story to be read to or with children. Stories can help children learn to cope with life's difficult situations. It is our intent that those who read or listen to this story will learn a number of things about how children react to divorce:

☐ It is common for them to experience a variety of feelings toward themselves and their parents, including anger, fear, insecurity, apathy and guilt.

☐ They often experience loss of appetite, have difficulty

falling asleep at night, shy away from friends and feel as if their lives are beginning to crumble.

☐ They may feel that their behavior had a lot to do with their parents' divorce.

☐ A child often tries to take on the responsibility of putting the parents' marriage back together.

☐ The acute pain of divorce usually subsides with time.

☐ Parental responsibilities change after a divorce. Some parents have more time to spend with their children and some have less time, but that is not necessarily to be equated with who is doing the better job of parenting.

☐ Parents may try to get children to tattle on the other parent—an extremely difficult position for a child.

☐ God gives each of us a great deal of freedom to choose how to live our own life—and people, including parents, don't always make the wisest choices.

☐ God does not always answer prayers the way we want them to be answered.

Ideally, this story should be read with one or both of the parents present. In that way, children will feel that their parents are sharing in some of their painful feelings, perceptions and experiences related to the divorce. With younger children, the story can be read in several segments as indicated. If an older child does not wish to read with either parent present, the parents should offer to talk about the story afterward. And who knows, even you as a parent may learn something from Rob's story.

Something to Cry About

Rob had his mom's curly brown hair and his dad's blue eyes and freckles. His mom's nose and his dad's chin. They teased him that he had one ear from each of them. He had his mom's maiden name, Lee, for his middle name, and his dad's last name for his last name. And his first name was one they'd both decided on when he was born. Rob liked it that way. He always knew he belonged to both his mom and his dad.

Since today was Saturday, Rob's mom had made hamburgers for lunch, but Rob wasn't eating much. He had taken only a couple of bites, and picked at his potato chips. Rob kept looking at the end of the table where his dad used to sit. His dad hadn't been sitting there for the last few weeks. It was so strange to have just the two of them there, where before it had always been all three of them together except when his dad was on some kind of trip. Rob's dad wasn't on a trip, though. His mom and dad had decided to get a divorce.

They had told him on a Saturday afternoon like this one nearly three weeks ago. What getting divorced meant, his dad said, was that he would be living in an apartment of his own in another neighborhood. He would come over to see Rob or else Rob could come over to see him once a week or maybe more often. But his dad would never live in the same house with them like before. Rob had started crying, even though he was already in the fifth grade and tall for his age. He had been crying a lot since then. Sometimes his mom looked as if she had been crying too.

Right now at the table, she looked worried and kind of annoyed. "Come on," she said, "hamburgers are your favorite, aren't they?"

"Yeah," Rob said.

"Well?" his mom said.

"Can I go out and play?" asked Rob.

His mother sighed. "Yes, you may be excused."

Rob didn't want to find any of his friends and see if they could play. It wasn't that there weren't other kids at school whose parents didn't live together. He remembered last year when his friend Kenny had announced that his parents were getting a divorce. Rob had felt bad, even a little sick to his stomach. He had thought, "Thank goodness, my parents are happy together. Our family would never do that." But even though Rob wasn't the only one, he still felt funny. These days he mostly wanted to be by himself. He had been spending a lot of time just riding around on his old blue Schwinn and thinking. Today, though, he felt that he needed to talk to someone. Maybe Ben was home.

Last year when Rob was in fourth grade, Ben was his Sunday-school teacher. Rob had another teacher this year. Now he and Ben were just friends. Ben was a lot older—he went to a place called a graduate school—but he was a good guy to talk to and he lived nearby, just a couple of blocks down Greenwood Street. Rob rode over there in a few minutes. It was the first really sunny day of spring, and on the way Rob noticed a whole bank of big red tulips in bloom, but even that didn't cheer him up.

There was no answer at the door, so Rob locked his bike and went around to the back yard. There was Ben, pulling weeds out from around a rose bush. Ben's aunt owned the house, but she was gone on a long trip, so Ben was living there and taking care of a yard full of rosebushes and a house full of African violets. From the back, Rob could see only the seat of Ben's work pants and the back of his wavy blonde hair. Ben's black cat, Chrysostom, was sitting nearby, purring in the sunshine. Chrysostom got named when Ben thought his new kitten was a *he,* and the name had stuck. It had stuck a long time: Chrysostom was twelve now, almost a year older than Rob. She saw Rob come through the open gate but was too comfortable to get up and greet him.

"Hi, Ben."

Ben turned around, a trowel in one hand and a clump of dandelions in the other. "Hey, Rob! How are you doing?"

"Okay." Rob flopped down on the grass and sat there frowning.

"You sure you're okay, Rob? You look a little down."

"Yeah, I guess I am. Remember I told you about how my mom and dad were getting a divorce?"

Ben stopped weeding. "Sure I remember."

"Well," said Rob, "it makes me feel really bad whenever I think about it. And I think about it all the time."

"I can see why," said Ben. "A divorce is a pretty tough thing to go through."

Rob nodded. "It's really weird."

"How do you mean?" Ben asked. He came over and sat down crosslegged near Rob.

"Well, I don't feel much like eating, even when Mom makes hamburgers or when I go out to eat with Dad. At night it's hard to go to sleep. And during the day it's sort of like I'm always tired, but it's just that I don't feel much like doing anything around the house or with the other kids." When Rob sighed he could smell the garden dirt and the grass, but he didn't enjoy it the way he usually did. "I just feel bad in a lot of ways." He raised his voice: "And I wish I didn't!"

Ben was nodding. "That's how it is with feelings. You can wish the feelings weren't there but they *are* and you can't make them go away."

"That doesn't seem fair," Rob said.

Ben looked as if he was trying to remember something. He said, "You know how last year in class we talked about God creating us?" Rob nodded. "Well, God made us so we can think thoughts and also feel feelings. The feelings are as important a part as the rest of us. I'd be surprised if you were feeling really happy right now or if you weren't thinking a lot about your family. I'd be surprised, and I'd also be worried about you. When there are things for you to feel sad about, you need to go ahead and have sad feelings. And when people feel really sad, sometimes they lose their appetite or have a hard time falling asleep at night. It's just normal to do some moping around."

Rob seemed surprised. "It is?"

"You bet it is," Ben said.

"That makes me feel a little better, Ben." They sat without talking for a minute. The only sounds were Chrysostom purring with half-closed eyes and an occasional squawk from a blue jay that she was pretending to ignore. Rob was frowning hard.

"Have you just felt sad," asked Ben, "or are you feeling angry too?"

"Yeah," Rob said. "Sometimes I feel really mad. And that's bad—you're not supposed to feel mad, especially at your mom and dad." Rob pulled up a fistful of grass. "And I feel like a big dumb baby for crying so much!"

"Hey, listen, Rob, those feelings are okay too. There's no reason to feel ashamed of crying—not when you have something to cry about. And I can see why you're angry. Anybody in your shoes would be. Nobody wants their parents to live apart from them—it would be best if all families lived together."

Rob looked up at the blue jay that was now scolding loudly from its safe perch in the spruce tree. "So you think it's okay that I feel like this?"

"Sure, it's okay. Now, if you felt this way for the rest of your life, that wouldn't be so good. For right now, you're sad, and it's fine to feel that. I'd feel pretty sad right now if I were you."

Rob sighed a great big sigh.

"Hey, Rob, you know they say that time has a way

99

of healing things, and I think that's true."

Rob sat up a little straighter. "You mean my dad might come back?"

"Well, no," Ben said. "There's a good chance he won't. But even if he doesn't, a lot of your feelings will go away after awhile. Pretty soon you won't be quite so sad and angry or be crying so much—and I bet your mom's hamburgers will start tasting great again."

Rob shook his head. "I don't feel like I'll ever be happy."

Ben didn't say anything at first. "Maybe I can show you what I mean," he said. "Remember Abbie?" Abbie had been Rob's black cocker spaniel.

"Yeah," said Rob.

"Remember how when she was hit by the car you cried and cried?" Rob nodded. "You're not so sad about Abbie now, are you?"

"No. That seems like a long time ago."

"That's what I mean. With time, things don't hurt so much."

"But that's different from my mom and dad getting a divorce."

"You're right," Ben said, "but there's something that's the same. When Abbie died, you lost her. You couldn't play with her anymore, or see her around the house. You still get to see your dad, but he's not around the way he used to be. I know your mom and dad are a whole lot more important than Abbie, but still, after a while you won't be feeling as bad as you feel right now. That's something I think you can look forward to, Rob. Like the song says: 'a time to weep, and a time to laugh. . . .' And speaking of time," Ben said, "I think it's time we went inside and got ourselves some apple juice. What do you say?"

* * *

The next week in Sunday school Rob's teacher told their class about prayer. He talked about how God wanted people to pray and say what they were thinking about and ask for what they needed. God answers prayer, the teacher said.

When Rob and his mother got home from church, he went into his room and shut the door. At church they sat down when they prayed, but Rob wanted God to know he was really serious. He knelt down beside his bed the way he'd seen in pictures, and whispered so that his mom wouldn't hear him. He figured God would be able to hear him okay since his teacher had said God heard even the thoughts inside your head. Rob knew exactly what he wanted to ask for.

"Please," he said, "put my family back together again like we used to be."

When his mom called him for lunch, Rob half expected to find his father sitting there at the table. Lunch was tuna casserole, but it was just Rob and his mom who ate it.

One day after school about a month later, Rob was riding around the neighborhood and decided to go by Ben's house. He left his bike in the yard and climbed the porch steps and knocked. Ben looked glad to see him when he opened the door.

101

"Rob, hi. Good to see you. Come on in." Rob liked the inside of Ben's house: it smelled like old books and spices.

"How about a cup of cocoa?" Ben offered. "It's a little chilly today."

"No, thanks, I just came to talk. Ben, can I ask you some things?"

"Sure, let's sit down."

Ben's living room was full of rocking chairs of all different shapes and sizes. Ben chose a squatty one with green striped upholstery. Rob settled himself in a tall one with a wicker seat and said, "Well, y'know how God answers prayer?" Ben nodded. "So I've been praying that God would let us be happy together again, my family, but my dad still hasn't come back. I've been praying really hard for a long time—" He counted the days on his fingers while Ben waited. "For nearly four weeks now and nothing's happened."

"Hmmm," Ben said. "Prayer can be hard to understand."

"But if God answers prayer," said Rob, "what's hard to understand?"

"It has to do with the freedom that God gives us. When we were created, God gave us the freedom to do things that are good for us or bad for us, right or wrong. Do you know what *freedom* means?"

"Freedom makes me think of someone getting out of jail," Rob said. "I guess I'm not sure I know exactly the way you mean it."

Ben explained: "When I say freedom I mean the choice we have about what we do and how we do it. I bet your parents pray that you would be good. Sometimes, though, you don't act like such a good kid. Sometimes, even though you know what you ought to be doing, you decide to do something else. Isn't that the way it is?"

Rob thought about how his mom had asked him to take out the garbage before he went out to ride his bike today and how he hadn't wanted to and had just not done it. "Yeah," Rob said.

"And I bet your parents are pretty glad when you are good. Because they know you're trying hard to please them and to please God.

"Well, what if God just *made* you be good and you didn't have any choice in the matter? It wouldn't mean much to your parents since it wouldn't be because you were *wanting* to be good and putting out any effort.

"Freedom is sort of like that: God gave your parents the freedom to love each other or not to love each other. They have the freedom to want to live together or not live together. Parents have to make that kind of decision on their own. God won't interfere and try to make them change their minds: God wants people to exercise their freedom."

"That makes sense," Rob said.

"So it isn't that God isn't answering your prayers, Rob —but maybe God's answer to your prayer is that your mom and dad have to make their own choice." Ben noticed that Rob's chair was rocking back and forth pretty fast, and Rob's nose was wrinkled up. "That's probably not the kind of answer you wanted to hear, huh?"

"No," Rob said, "it sure wasn't."

"Most of the time," said Ben, "kids just don't have much say-so in what their parents do. Adults have to decide how they want to live. That's not a very pleasant answer for you. It's not so pleasant for your mom and dad either. They not only have the freedom to make their own decisions, they have to live with the results of those decisions." Rob hadn't thought about its being hard for his parents.

"Your folks decided to get a divorce, and I'm sure they'll be happier now in some ways. They won't have all the arguments they used to have. And that's probably a good thing. But they'll be less happy in some other ways. I bet your dad isn't too glad about living all alone in an apartment. He'll get lonely without you and your mom there. And your mom has a lot of extra work to do around the house without your dad. She had to go out and find an accounting job five days a week to support you two, and I bet that's pretty hard on her. Freedom costs something. When your parents decided to get divorced, they decided they were willing to pay the price that went with it."

Rob was staring down at Ben's carpet. In a quiet voice he said, "I guess I'll quit praying then."

"You know what, Rob, I can think of something you could pray for that would really help things with your parents."

Rob looked up surprised. "What's that?"

"You could pray that your mom and dad would feel accepted by God."

"What does that mean?" Rob asked.

"Well, a lot of times parents who get divorced feel pretty guilty. They know it's hard on their kids, not to mention hard on themselves, and they feel real bad about it. Divorced parents can start not liking themselves. And when you don't like yourself, it's hard to believe that God still likes you and loves you. God doesn't change like that, though. God loved your mom and dad before they were ever your mom and dad, and while they were married, and now that they're separated. Your parents need to understand and believe that God still loves and accepts them no matter what."

Rob rocked for a while without saying anything. Finally he said, "Okay, Ben, I guess I'll keep praying after all."

* * *

When Rob came into the house his mom was standing in the kitchen doorway, her arms folded across her chest. "Rob, do you remember that I asked you to take out the garbage?"

Now Rob remembered. "I guess I forgot, Mom."

"This is the third time in a row you've forgotten," she said. "You also forgot to straighten up your room."

"Sorry, Mom."

"Would you go do that now, please?"

"Aww, Mom, I was going to ride down to the park and—"

"If you hurry and clean your room," she broke in, "you'll still have time to do that too before supper."

"But Mom—"

"No but-moms," she said, "just get going."

On the way to his room Rob dragged his feet as if he was walking through cement. When he finally got there, he looked around at the model airplanes and books and clothes and his rock collection scattered around the floor. "I don't see what needs cleaning," he said, but not quite loud enough for his mom to hear. He kicked a tennis shoe into his closet, then shut the door and sank down on his bed. "I wish I were with Dad," he muttered. "We'd go for a hike or to a baseball game instead of all this." Rob reached underneath himself and pulled the other tennis shoe out from the covers where it had been poking his ribs. He held it in front of him. "Dad," he told it, "doesn't make me take out the garbage." Rob tossed the shoe across the room and wondered if Ben would understand why it was that his mom was getting meaner and meaner while his dad was getting nicer and nicer.

The next day after school Rob's mom was still at work. So Rob answered the door and found Ben smiling down at him.

"How are you doing, Rob? I thought I'd stop by and catch up on things."

"Come on in, Ben. I was just thinking about you."

"Oh, about what?" Ben asked, pulling up a chair at the kitchen table. Rob sat down too.

"I don't understand the way my mom and dad are

changing. My mom and I used to spend time together and do things, and now all she ever does is tell me to take out the garbage or pick up my clothes. Or take a bath when I just had one or go to bed when it's not even my real bedtime yet."

"How about your dad?"

"It's just the other way with him," Rob said. "He used to be at work all the time and busy doing stuff around the house on weekends. But now we go places together on weekends all the time. Last week we went to the zoo, and he let me stay in the snake house as long as I wanted. We do fun things together."

"You know, Rob, I bet a lot of kids feel that way when their parents separate. You and your dad have only a little time to spend together each week, so when you *are* together you do mostly fun things. But you live with your mom, and that means she might ask you to help fold the laundry or wash dishes."

"And set the table and sweep the porch and—" Rob began.

Ben laughed and held up his hand. "Okay, okay, I get the idea," he said. "But what do you suppose it would be like if it was the other way around? What if your mom had moved into an apartment and you lived with your dad at home?"

Rob put his chin in his hand. "Yeah," he said. "I guess then I'd do fun things with my mom on weekends and holidays, and dad would make me help with chores around the house. I guess it isn't really that my mom's

107

gotten meaner and my dad's gotten nicer."

"I think you're right," Ben agreed. "Their responsibilities have just changed. Your mom has a full-time job now, and that's besides keeping the house clean and getting you off to school in the mornings and shopping for groceries and . . ." He stopped talking, out of breath. "She's pretty busy, it sounds like. Probably she could use a lot more of your help now that your dad's not around the house." Rob didn't say anything. Ben said, "Can I ask you something, Rob?" The boy nodded. "Have you been feeling kind of cranky about having to help out?" Rob nodded again. "And has your mom had to discipline you to get you to help?"

Rob sighed. "Yeah," he said.

"Do you suppose," Ben went on, "you might be able to help your mom around the house without her always having to ask? And when you do, try to remember that maybe she's having a pretty hard time herself, and that she still loves you a lot, just the way you know your dad does."

"Yeah," Rob said, "I'll try."

Ben looked at his watch. "Well, right now I have to go. But I've got some errands to run tomorrow afternoon. Why don't you ask your mom if you could help me after school?"

"Okay," Rob said. "Thanks for talking."

* * *

The next day at school, Rob wasn't paying much attention to what the teacher said about spelling and long division.

He was thinking about how he'd acted at home the last several months. He'd made his mom pretty impatient sometimes. He thought of ways he could be good—turn off the TV the first time she asked; come when he was called; remember to feed Mickey and Minnie, the goldfish. . . . Some of the things he thought of that he needed to do better were things he'd never been good about doing. Rob had always hated making his bed. What good was all that smoothing and tucking-in when you were just going to mess it up that night? He remembered how sometimes his mom and dad used to argue about whether or not he should have to make his bed.

By the time school got out, Rob was really disgusted. He stomped toward Ben's house, kicking any rocks on the sidewalk out of the way. One rock he kicked was so big that it hurt his toe. "Ow!" he said, and thought to himself, "Serves you right!"

He took the short cut through the park. Sam and Kenny and some of the other kids were on the field, kicking around a soccer ball. Sam saw him first: "Hey, Rob!" The others looked in the direction Sam had yelled. The chorus began: "Rob!" "Hi, Rob!" "C'mon and play!" "You can be on my team." "No, you got last pick, Rob's on my team!" "Come on, Rob!"

Rob waved but kept walking. "I can't," he shouted back, "I have to go."

He heard their groans behind him, but he wasn't about to stop and have a good time.

When he got to Ben's house, Ben wasn't home yet,

109

so Rob sat down on his front porch to wait. He took off his left shoe (he always kicked with his left foot) to see if he was going to get a bruise. Sure enough, the end of his big toe was turning purplish. It still hurt. "It *does* serve you right!" This time he said it aloud. Chrysostom came meowing out from under the porch. She tried to rub her head against Rob's foot, but he shooed her away.

Ben walked up just as Rob was tying his shoelace. They both waved. "Been waiting long?" asked Ben.

"No, just a few minutes."

"Good. I was at the library looking up some books for a paper I'm writing."

"Do you have to do homework too?" Rob asked.

"Boy, do I ever," Ben said. He had a backpack over his shoulder and jiggled it a little to show how full it was of papers and heavy books.

Rob nodded. "At school we had to write a report on what we did over our Easter vacation. What's yours about, Ben?"

"Well," Ben said. "It might be kind of hard to describe. Let's get in the car and go. Basically, this paper is going to talk about how certain chemicals affect plants."

"That sounds interesting," Rob said, remembering his manners as he slammed the door shut.

"Well, I hope my professor likes it." Ben started the engine. "Thought any more about doing chores at home?"

"Yeah," Rob said looking out the window as the houses passed by. "I figured something out."

"What have you figured out?"

Rob said, "It's my fault."

"What's your fault?"

"It's all my fault," Rob said. Ben looked puzzled as he watched the road ahead, so Rob said what he had sort of thought before but was sure of now. "Well, you know how we were talking about how everybody has the freedom to be good or bad?" Ben nodded. "I've been really bad. And my parents' getting a divorce is my fault."

"How do you figure that?" Ben said.

"I didn't do a lot of the stuff I was supposed to. And I'd complain about having to scrub out the tub when none of the other guys I know have to. Well, almost none. And if my mom and dad wouldn't let me spend a school night at my friend's house I'd argue about it with them. Then sometimes they'd start arguing with each other."

Ben had been shaking his head that he didn't understand, but now he was shaking his head no. "A lot of kids," he said, "probably think it's their fault when their parents split up."

Rob knew that Ben got to talk to a lot of kids. During summers Ben went up to Deer Lake to be a counselor at the camps they had there. Now Rob wanted to believe what Ben was saying but he couldn't quite do it. "But don't you think my mom and dad would've stayed together if I'd been better?"

"No, I really don't, Rob. Look at all the mothers and fathers who have great marriages and whose kids are terrors. Look at all the parents who have unhappy mar-

111

riages and also have really well-behaved kids." Rob could think of both kinds of families in his neighborhood. "You know, Rob, I think it's safe to say that even if you'd been a perfect angel all the time, your parents probably would have still decided to get divorced."

"Are you sure?" Rob asked. "Even if I did everything they told me and never made them have to yell at me?"

"I think so, Rob." The boy didn't say any more. "You know what else I think?"

"No, what?"

"I think we should stop for a snack before we go to the hardware store." Ben turned into a parking lot and got out.

All of a sudden Rob realized he was hungry. Usually he'd have some cookies and milk or an apple after he got home from school. "That sounds good," he said and followed Ben to his favorite ice cream place.

Rob got two scoops and Ben ordered a malt. They talked about the games Rob and his dad played on the computer his dad owned, and about the computer Ben used in the lab to help him with his school work.

Rob took a last bite and wiped away his white mustache with the back of his hand. His toe didn't hurt so much now. The boy let out a deep breath. "I'm sure glad," he told Ben, "that it's not my fault." Ben smiled.

Rob jumped out of the car when Ben took him home and hardly said good-bye as he ran for the front door: he had forgotten to feed the goldfish that morning.

* * *

Supper that night was pork chops and jello salad with

carrots. After brownies for dessert, Rob volunteered not only to wash but also to dry the dishes. His mom seemed a little surprised, but thanked him and went into the living room to read the evening paper. When Rob was done he came in and asked for the comics. They'd been sitting quietly reading for about five minutes when Rob laid down the comics and said, "Mom?"

"What, honey?" she said.

"Do you think we could have a picnic at Lincoln Park next Saturday if it's nice?"

She smiled. "Sure, Rob, I don't see why not. That sounds like fun."

They both started reading again. Rob read Peanuts and Gasoline Alley and Family Circus, then laid down the comic page again. "Mom?"

"What, honey?"

"Don't you think it would be even funner if we asked Dad to go on the picnic with us? I think that would be really fun. And you know what, I think Dad even mentioned that he'd take me there on a picnic sometime, so wouldn't it be a good idea to have both picnics at once?"

Rob pretended not to see his mom's frown.

"You could make your special potato salad. And you know the way Dad can barbeque chicken so it tastes real good, and he's teaching me how to throw the frisbee so I can make it go practically as far as he does . . ." Rob's voice slowed down and faded out. "Well, what do you think, Mom?"

"I don't think that's a very good idea, honey."

113

"You don't? How come?"

"Think about it a minute, Rob, and see if you can tell me."

Rob thought for a second. He didn't need Ben to figure this one out for him. "Well, you and Dad are getting a divorce because you don't want to live with each other anymore. And if you don't want to live with each other anymore, I guess you probably don't even want to spend time with each other any more. Not even on a picnic. Right?"

"Right," his mom said. "Now, how about taking a bath?"

* * *

The next time Rob went to spend the weekend with his dad, they went out for ice cream sundaes after supper on Friday night. His dad said Rob could have anything on the menu, and he'd picked the Super-Duper Caramel-Coming-Out-Your-Ears Special. Back at the apartment, they played a new game on his dad's computer. When they got up the next morning, Rob's dad made pancakes in the shape of animals and let Rob try to make some too. Afterward, they played catch with the football and in the afternoon went to a carnival. Rob went on the roller coaster four times, and on the Ferris wheel, the Octopus, the Spinning Barrel, the Loop-the-loop, the Round-up and the Crazy Cars.

Tonight Rob and his dad were working together building a model of the Wright brothers' airplane. Rob had asked his dad who the Wright brothers were. His dad was a high-school history teacher and told him about Orville and Wilbur and how they made their first airplane in a bicycle repair shop in Ohio. Rob liked hearing about all that kind of stuff his dad knew. And Rob really liked it that his dad let him stay up late and had forgotten to make him wash his hands before supper.

Just as they were gluing on the propeller, Rob's dad said, "Is your mother taking good care of you?" At supper that night, he'd asked Rob, "What kind of food are you eating at home? Do you have meat for supper every night?"

This was the part of being with his dad that Rob didn't like at all. In fact, Rob was getting to hate it.

He wiggled around in his chair. "Mom takes good care of me, Dad."

"Well, I just wanted to make sure. Your mom isn't such a good mother sometimes—she's so forgetful."

Rob didn't say anything. It made him feel bad to hear his dad say things like that. He wasn't sure why. He guessed his mom was kind of forgetful—his dad ought to know, and he wouldn't tell him anything that wasn't true. But his mom really didn't seem any more forgetful than his dad.

Later, when his dad tucked him into the folded-out sofa bed, he said goodnight but still stayed sitting on the edge of the mattress. "Does your mother go out with any men, Rob?" he asked. Rob's dad had asked him that before—just like his mom had asked, "Does your dad talk about dating other women?" Rob always just said

115

he didn't know, and wished hard that they wouldn't keep asking.

On Sundays Rob's dad always dropped him off in front of their house, and his mom was always there waiting for him. This Sunday was just the same.

"Hi, honey," she said, and gave Rob a big hug. "Come sit down and tell me what you and your dad did together."

Rob told her about the carnival and model airplane—he thought maybe it would be best not to mention the huge caramel sundae.

"What time did you get to bed last night?" she asked.

"I don't know, Mom. We just went to bed when we got tired."

"Your father isn't careful enough with your bedtime," she said. "First thing you know you'll be getting too tired out and come down with flu." She felt Rob's forehead. "You seem a little flushed," she said. Rob felt his forehead. It didn't feel at all hot to him.

"I feel fine, Mom, really. Can I go out and ride my bike for a while?"

"All right. Be careful, though, and be sure you're home in time for supper."

"Okay," Rob said and went to get his bike out of the garage. He headed toward Ben's house, and in a few minutes was sitting on Ben's living room rug, drinking apple juice and telling about the way his weekends always seemed to go. Ben sat listening, petting Chrysostom who was sitting in his lap. Rob told about the questions his dad would ask him when Rob got to his apartment, and the same kind of questions his mom would ask him when he got home on Sundays.

"I'm not exactly sure why," Rob said, "but they don't seem like very nice questions. I guess what I mean is that they don't make me feel very good. They make me feel creepy."

"You're sort of in the middle between your mom and dad," Ben said. "And they're having a pretty big fight."

"That's sure what it feels like," Rob said. "They say other things too. Like last week my mom said she didn't think my dad loved me as much as she loved me."

"I'll tell you, Rob, that's a bum deal, but it's something that happens a lot when parents are divorced. It's like the mom and dad don't want to see each other, but they try to speak to each other through their kids."

"What do you mean, 'speak to each other through their kids'?"

"Your mom and dad both have some pretty angry feelings, but they don't want to talk to each other. So they end up telling you."

"They never say they're mad," Rob said.

"There are plenty of ways to say you're angry other than to come right out and say 'I'm mad,' " Ben said. "Another thing is that both your mom and dad want you to love them. Without even thinking about what they're doing, each might be trying to get you to like them better than the other one by saying those kinds of things."

"Is all that bad stuff the truth?"

"I can't tell you whether the bad things they say about

each other are true or not. Some things may be and others may not be.

"But I can tell you something you might do so you don't have to keep listening to the unpleasant things your folks have been saying."

"Do you mean *this?*" Rob asked, sticking his fingers in his ears.

Ben laughed and shook his head. Chrysostom woke up. She stepped out of Ben's lap and stretched herself long enough for two black cats, then walked over to Rob and settled herself into his lap. "What I was thinking, Rob, is, the next time your mom or dad asks you one of those questions that you don't like, or tells you something that you don't like about the other parent, why don't you just say that it makes you feel uncomfortable."

"Uncomfortable?" said Rob.

"That's a good way to put it: uncomfortable. That way you're not telling them they're doing something bad. You're just telling them that what they're saying makes you feel some way you'd rather not feel."

"Creepy," Rob said.

"Right," said Ben. "Do you see what I mean, Rob?"

Rob nodded as he sat rubbing Chrysostom under the chin. "I think so."

"Remember," Ben added, "it's okay to have feelings —even angry feelings. But when you have feelings you don't like, a lot of times it's a good idea to tell other people about it. I don't think your mom and dad realize how it hurts you to hear them talk like that. And I'll bet you they'll

118

do it a lot less after you talk to them about it."

"I sure hope so," said Rob.

"So do I," Ben said. "So do I."

Notes

Chapter 1

[1] L. Francke et al., "The Children of Divorce," *Newsweek*, 11 February 1980, p. 58.

[2] Robert Kelly, *Courtship, Marriage and the Family* (New York: Harcourt Brace Jovanovich, 1979), p. 583.

[3] E. Golanty and B. Harris, *Marriage and Family Life* (Boston: Houghton Mifflin, 1982), p. 5.

[4] J. Wallerstein and J. Kelly, "Children and Divorce: A Review," *Social Work*, November 1979, pp. 468-75.

Chapter 2

[1] Richard Gardner, *Psychotherapy with Children of Divorce* (New York: Jason Aronson, 1976), p. 24.

[2] Wallerstein and Kelly, "Children and Divorce," p. 471.

[3] Graham Blaine, Jr., "The Effect of Divorce upon the Personality Development of Children and Youth," in *Explaining Divorce to Children*, ed. Earl A. Grollman (Boston: Beacon, 1969), p. 80.

[4] Carolyn Phillips, *Our Family Got a Divorce* (Glendale, Cal.: Regal, 1979), p. 227.

[5] Jerry Bigner, *Parent-Child Relations* (New York: Macmillan, 1979), p. 32.

[6] Blaine, "The Effect of Divorce," p. 78.

Chapter 3
[1]Wallerstein and Kelly, "Children and Divorce," p. 469.
[2]Gardner, *Psychotherapy*, p. 248.
[3]Wallerstein and Kelly, "Children and Divorce," p. 469.
[4]M. Hetherington, M. Cox and R. Cox, "The Aftermath of Divorce," in *Mother-Child, Father-Child Relations*, ed. Joseph H. Stevens, Jr., and Marilyn Matthews (Washington, D.C.: National Association for the Education of Young Children, 1977), p. 33.
[5]J. McDermott, "Parental Divorce in Early Childhood," *American Journal of Psychiatry* 124, no. 10 (April 1968), p. 120.
[6]Lora Tessman, *Children of Parting Parents* (New York: Jason Aronson, 1978), p. 132.
[7]Wallerstein and Kelly, "Children and Divorce," p. 470.

Chapter 5
[1]Marshall Hamilton, *Fathers' Influence on Children* (Chicago: Nelson Hall, 1977), p. 51.
[2]Hetherington, Cox and Cox, "The Aftermath of Divorce," p. 21.

Chapter 6
[1]Tessman, *Children of Parting Parents*, p. 331.
[2]J. Wallerstein and J. Kelly, "The Effects of Parental Divorce: The Adolescent Experience," in *The Child in His Family*, ed. E. James Anthony and Cyrille Koupernik, vol. 3 (New York: John Wiley and Sons, 1974), p. 488.
[3]Ibid., p. 481, and Hamilton, *Father's Influence*, p. 25.
[4]A. Ritchie and A. Deirono, "Family Therapy in the Treatment of Adolescents with Divorced Parents," in *Therapeutic Needs of the Family: Problems, Descriptions and Therapeutic Approaches*, ed. E. Richard (Springfield, Ill.: Thomas, 1974).

Chapter 7
[1]Wallerstein and Kelly, "Children and Divorce," p. 472.
[2]Ibid.
[3]McDermott, "Parental Divorce," p. 119.
[4]L. Ames, "Children and Divorce: What the Teacher Can Do," *Educational Digest*, November 1969, p. 20.

Recommended Reading

Ames, L. "Children and Divorce: What the Teacher Can Do." *Educational Digest,* November 1969, pp. 19-21.
   Particularly oriented to professional educators.
Elkind, David. *The Child's Reality: Three Developmental Themes.* Hillsdale, N.J.: Lawrence Erlbaum Associates, 1978.
   Helps parents understand how children construct reality out of their experience with the environment. While the three developmental themes referred to in the book's title—religious development, perceptual development and egocentrism—do not all focus on divorce, they can help parents better understand their child's reactions and questions concerning the divorce.
Francke, L. and Reese, M. "The Child of Divorce." *Newsweek,* 11 February 1980, pp. 58-60.
   Good overview.
Gardner, Richard A. *Psychotherapy with Children of Divorce.* New York: Jason Aronson, Inc., 1976.
   A 534-page volume, well written and insightful, especially oriented to therapists. Gardner has also written *The Boys and Girls Book about Divorce* (same publisher), excellent for children.
Greif, Judith B. "Fathers, Children and Joint Custody." *American Journal of Psychiatry* 49 (1979):311-19.
   Encourages joint custody arrangements, citing that children of di-

vorce, as do children of intact families, need loving relationships with two parents.

Grollman, Earl A., ed. *Explaining Divorce to Children.* Boston: Beacon Press, 1969.

Chapters by authorities on various aspects of how divorce affects children, drawing from much useful research. Chapters on the views of a minister, a priest and a rabbi.

Grollman, Earl A. *Talking about Divorce and Separation.* Boston: Beacon Press, 1975.

Written for children in story form. Questions and explanations for adults also.

Hetherington, E. M.; Cox, M.; and Cox, R. "The Aftermath of Divorce." In *Mother-Child, Father-Child Relations,* ed. Joseph H. Stevens and Marilyn Matthews. Washington, D.C.: National Association for the Education of Young Children, 1977.

Hetherington, E. M. "Divorce: A Child's Perspective." *American Psychologist* 34:851-58.

Overview of divorce and its impact on children, with research findings.

Kalter, N., and Rembar, J. "The Significance of a Child's Age at the Time of Parental Divorce." *American Journal of Orthopsychiatry* 51 (1981):85-100.

Looks at the different constellations of emotional-behavioral difficulties associated with children's ages at divorce.

Muuss, Robert E., ed. *Adolescent Behavior and Society: A Book of Readings.* New York: Random House, 1975.

Fifty-six articles ranging in content from the formation of self-identity to moral development, and from the adolescent's interaction with his family to adjustment at school. This book can increase parents' sensitivity to the needs and problems of their adolescent.

Narramore, S. Bruce. *Adolescence Is Not an Illness.* Old Tappan, N.J.: Fleming Revell, 1980.

Background for understanding the adolescent so that divorce can be viewed with this general knowledge in mind.

Phillips, C. *Our Family Got a Divorce.* Glendale, Cal.: Regal Books, 1979.

Delightful story for children to help them better understand what they are going through. The book's tone is encouraging and points to healing through a relationship with Christ.

Swihart, P. *How to Live with Your Feelings.* Downers Grove, Ill.: Inter-Varsity Press, 1976.
Helpful information on emotions for parents dealing with their own feelings as well as their children's.

Tessman, Lora. *Children of Parting Parents.* New York: Jason Aronson, 1978.
A fairly technical yet well-written book of most use to professional counselors.

Visher, E., and Visher, J. *Step Families.* New York: Brunner/Mazel, 1979.
Helpful information on adjustment of children in remarriage, although not written from a Christian world view.

Wallerstein, J., and Kelly, J. "Children and Divorce: A Review." *Social Work,* November 1979, pp. 468-75.
Excellent review of lengthy research.

Wallerstein, J., and Kelly, J. "Effects of Parental Divorce: The Adolescent Experience." In *The Child in His Family,* ed. E. James Anthony and Cyrille Koupernik. New York: John Wiley & Sons, 1974, pp. 479-505.